Last Stop
Auschwitz

www.penguin.co.uk

Last Stop Auschwitz

My story of survival
from within the camp

Eddy de Wind

Translated from the Dutch
by David Colmer

BLACK SWAN

TRANSWORLD PUBLISHERS
61–63 Uxbridge Road, London W5 5SA
www.penguin.co.uk

Transworld is part of the Penguin Random House group of companies
whose addresses can be found at global.penguinrandomhouse.com

Originally published in Dutch as *Eindstation Auschwitz*, 1946
First published in Great Britain in 2020 by Doubleday
an imprint of Transworld Publishers
Black Swan edition published 2020

This publication has been made possible with financial support
from the Dutch Foundation for Literature.

Nederlands
letterenfonds
dutch foundation
for literature

A CIP catalogue record for this book is available from the British Library.

ISBN 9781784164980

Typeset in 10.34/14.33pt Sabon Next LT Pro
by Integra Software Services Pvt. Ltd, Pondicherry.

Printed and bound in Great Britain by Clays Ltd, Elcograf S.p.A.

Penguin Random House is committed to a sustainable future for
our business, our readers and our planet. This book is made
from Forest Stewardship Council® certified paper.

3 5 7 9 10 8 6 4 2

Contents

Eddy and Friedel on their wedding day in Westerbork, May 1943.
They are surrounded by prominent residents, colleagues and
friends from the camp.

*I*N 1943, JEWISH DOCTOR EDDY DE WIND *volunteered to work in Westerbork, a transit camp for the deportation of Jews in the east of the Netherlands. From Westerbork inmates were sent on to concentration camps, including Auschwitz and Bergen-Belsen. Eddy had been told that his mother would be exempted from deportation in exchange for his work – in fact she had already been sent to Auschwitz. At Westerbork, Eddy met a young Jewish nurse called Friedel. They fell in love and married at the camp.*

In 1943, they too were transported to Auschwitz and were separated: Eddy ended up in Block 9 as part of the medical staff, Friedel in Block 10, where sterilization and other barbaric medical experiments were conducted by the notorious Josef Mengele and the gynaecologist Carl Clauberg.

Somehow, both Eddy and Friedel survived.

When the Russians approached Auschwitz in the autumn of 1944, the Nazis tried to cover their tracks. They fled, marching their many prisoners, including Friedel, towards Germany. These Death Marches were intended to eradicate all evidence of the concentration camp's atrocities.

Eddy hid and remained in the camp; it would take months before the war ended. He joined the Russian liberators. By day, he treated the often very ill survivors the Nazis had left behind and also Russian soldiers. By night, having found a pencil and notebook, he began to write with furious energy about his experiences at Auschwitz.

In his traumatized state, he created the character of Hans to be the narrator of his own story. Other than in a few instances, the horror of his experience was still so raw he couldn't find the words to describe it in the first person.

This is Eddy's story.

HOW FAR IS IT to those hazy blue mountains? How wide is the plain that stretches out in the radiant spring sunshine? It's a day's march for feet that are free. A single hour on horseback at full trot. For us it is further, much further, infinitely far. Those mountains are not of this world, not of our world. Because between us and those mountains is the wire.

Our yearning, the wild pounding of our hearts, the blood that rushes to our heads – they are all powerless. Because of that wire between us and the plain. Two parallel fences of high-voltage barbed wire with dim red lights that glow above them as a sign that death is lurking there, lying in wait for all of us imprisoned here in this rectangle enclosed by a tall white wall.

Always the same image, the same feeling. We stand at the windows of our *blocks* and look into the enticing distance while our chests heave with tension and impotence. We are ten metres away from each other. I lean out of the window while longing for that faraway freedom. Friedel can't even do that, her imprisonment is more complete. I can still move freely through the *Lager*. Friedel can't even do that.

I live in Block 9, an ordinary hospital block. Friedel lives in Block 10. There are sick people there too, but not like in my block. Where I am, there are people who have fallen ill from cruelty, starvation and overwork. Those are natural causes that lead to natural diseases that can be diagnosed.

1

Block 10 is the experimental block. The women who live there have been violated by sadists who call themselves professors, violated in a way that a woman has never been violated before, violated in the most beautiful thing they possess: their womanhood, their ability to become mothers.

A girl who is forced to submit to an uncontrolled brute's savage lust suffers too, but the deed she endures springs from life itself, from life's urges. In Block 10 the motive is not an eruption of desire – it is a political delusion, a financial interest.

All this we know as we look out over this plain in the south of Poland and long to run through the fields and marshes that separate us from the hazy blue Beskid Mountains on the horizon. But that is not all we know. We also know that for us there is only one end, only one way to be free from this barbed-wire hell: death.

We know that death can come to us here in different forms.

He can come as an honourable foe that a doctor can fight. Even if this death has base allies – hunger, cold, fleas and lice – it remains a natural death that can be classified according to an official cause. But he won't come to us like that. He will come to us just as he came to those millions who have preceded us here. When he comes, he will almost certainly be stealthy and invisible, almost odourless even.

We know that only subterfuge hides death from our view. We know that this death is uniformed because the gas tap is operated by a man in uniform: SS.

That is why we yearn so, looking out at those hazy blue mountains, which are just thirty-five kilometres away, but for us eternally unattainable.

That is why I lean so far out of the window towards Block 10, where she is standing.

That is why her hands grip the wire mesh on her window so tightly.

That is why she rests her head on the wood, because her longing for me must remain unquenched, along with our yearning for those tall, hazy blue mountains.

THE YOUNG GRASS, THE swollen brown chestnut buds and the radiant sun that was growing more glorious with every passing day seemed to promise new life. But the Earth was covered with the chill of death. It was spring 1943.

The Germans were deep in Russia and the fortunes of war had yet to turn.

In the West, the Allies still hadn't set foot on the Continent.

The terror raging over Europe was taking fiercer and fiercer forms.

The Jews were the conquerors' playthings. It was a game of cat and mouse. Night after night, motorbikes roared through the streets of Amsterdam, jackboots stamped and orders snarled along the once so-peaceful canals.

Then, later, in Westerbork, the mouse was often released for a moment. People were allowed to move freely around the camp, packages arrived and families stayed together. Everyone wrote an obedient 'I am fine' letter to Amsterdam, so that others in turn would also surrender peacefully to the *Grüne Polizei*.

In Westerbork the Jews were given the illusion that everything might not turn out too badly, that although they were now excluded from society, they would one day return from their isolation.

> *'When the war is done and everyone*
> *Is on the way back home …'*

was the start of a popular song.

Not only did they not see their future fate, there were even some who had the courage – or was it blindness? – to start a new life, to found a new family. Every day Dr Molhuijsen came to the camp on behalf of the mayor of the village of Westerbork, and one magnificent morning – from April's quota of nine fine days – Hans and Friedel appeared before him.

They were two idealists: he was twenty-seven and a well-known doctor at the camp; she was just eighteen. They had got to know each other in the ward where he held sway and she was a nurse.

> *'Because alone we are none,*
> *But together we are one.'*

he had written in a poem for her, and that was exactly how they felt. Together they would win through. Maybe they would manage to stay in Westerbork until the end of the war, and otherwise continue the struggle together in Poland. Because one day the war would end and a German victory was something nobody believed in.

They were together for half a year like this, living in the 'doctor's room', a cardboard box in the corner of a large barracks with one hundred and thirty women. They didn't have the room to themselves, but shared it with another doctor and, later, two other couples. Definitely not the appropriate surroundings for establishing a young married life together. But none of that would have mattered if there hadn't been a single *Transport*: one thousand people every Tuesday morning. Men and women, young and old, including babies and even people who were ill.

Only a very small number were allowed to stay behind, when Hans and the other doctors were able to prove that they were too sick to spend three days on a train. Also exempt were those with a privileged status: the baptized, the mixed marriages, *alte Kamp-Insassen* who had been interned since 1938, and permanent members of staff like Hans and Friedel.

There was a staff list of a thousand names, but there was also a steady influx of new arrivals from the cities who needed to be protected, sometimes on German orders, sometimes because they really had been worthy citizens, but mostly because of longstanding connections with the notables on the Jewish Council or with the alte Kamp-Insassen, who had a firm grip on the key positions in the camp. Then the list of one thousand would be revised.

This was how it came about that an employee of the Jewish Council came to Hans and Friedel on the night of Monday, 13 September 1943 to tell them that they had to get ready for deportation. Hans dressed quickly and made a round of all the authorities, who worked under high pressure on the night before the weekly transport. Dr Spanier, the head of the hospital, was furious. Hans had been in the camp for a year. He had worked hard; there were many others who had arrived later and never done a thing. But Hans was on the Jewish Council staff list and if they couldn't keep him on it, the health service couldn't do anything about it either.

At eight o'clock they were standing with all their belongings next to the train, which ran through the middle of the camp.

It was tremendously busy. The camp police and the men of the Flying Column were carrying baggage to the train and two wagons were loaded with provisions for the journey. The male nurses from the hospital came trailing up with the patients, mostly elderly, who couldn't walk. That wasn't sufficient reason to let them stay – next week they would be no more mobile than they were now. Also present were friends and family who were staying in the camp; they stood behind the cordon, twenty or thirty metres away from the train, often crying more than those who were leaving.

At the front and back of the train were carriages with SS guards, but they were very fair, and tried to keep people's spirits up, because it was essential to keep the Dutch from finding out how 'their' Jews were really being treated.

Half past ten: departure. The doors of the goods wagons were bolted on the outside. A last goodbye, a last wave through the hatches in the roof of the wagon, and then they were on their way to Poland, exact destination unknown.

Hans and Friedel had been lucky and were in a wagon with only young people, old friends of Friedel's from the Zionist group she had belonged to, friendly and accommodating. Altogether there were thirty-eight of them. That was relatively few and, with a little reorganization, hanging baggage from the ceiling, there was room for them to all sit down on the floor.

The fun and games started during the trip. At the first stop, SS men came into the wagon demanding their cigarettes, and later their watches. The next time it was fountain pens and jewellery. The lads laughed it off, giving them a few loose cigarettes and claiming it was all they had. A lot of them were originally German; they'd had dealings with the SS often enough before. They'd come through it alive then too, and they weren't going to let themselves be bullied around this time either.

They weren't given any food in those three days and they never saw the train's provisions again. But that didn't matter! They still had enough with them from Westerbork. Now and then a couple of them were allowed to leave the wagon to empty the small and overflowing toilet barrel. They were delighted when they saw signs of bombing raids in the cities, but otherwise the trip was uneventful. On the third day they found out their destination: Auschwitz. It was just a meaningless word, neither good nor bad.

That night they reached the Auschwitz railway yard.

THE TRAIN STOOD STILL for a long time – so long they grew impatient and wished they would finally get some clarity, that they would finally see what Auschwitz was. The clarity came.

At the first sign of dawn, the train started moving for the last time, only to stop again a few minutes later at an embankment in the middle of flat countryside. Standing beside the embankment were groups of ten to twelve men. They were dressed in blue-and-white-striped clothes with matching hats. A great number of SS men were walking back and forth in an incomprehensible flurry of activity.

The moment the train was at a standstill, the costumed men stormed up to the wagons and pulled the doors open. 'Throw out the baggage. In front of the wagon. All of it.' They were terribly shocked because they realized they had now lost everything. Quickly they tried to slip the most essential items under their clothes, but the men had already leapt into the wagons and begun tossing out baggage and people. All at once they were outside, where they hesitated for a moment. But that hesitation didn't last long. SS men came at them from all sides, pushing them towards a road that ran parallel to the railway track, and kicking anyone who didn't move fast enough or hitting them with their sticks, so that everyone hurried as quickly as they possibly could to join the long lines that were forming.

Only then did Hans know for certain that the two of them were going to be split up, that men and women were being separated. He hurried to kiss Friedel – 'Till we meet again' – and then it was over. An officer with a stick was standing at the front of the lines as they slowly marched towards him. He cast a fleeting glance at each person and pointed with his stick: 'Left. Right.' Old men, invalids and boys up to about eighteen went left. The young and sturdy went right.

Hans reached the officer, but wasn't paying attention. He only had eyes for Friedel, who was standing in her line a few metres away and waiting until it was the women's turn. She smiled at him as if to say, *Be patient, it will be all right*. That was why he didn't hear the officer – who was a doctor – ask him how old he was. Annoyed at not being answered, the doctor gave Hans a blow with his stick that immediately sent him flying to the left.

He was standing among the weak and infirm: old men, a blind man next to him and a youth on the other side who looked like an imbecile. Hans bit his lip with fear. He realized that only the strong stood any chance of staying alive and he didn't want to share the fate of the children and the elderly. But it wasn't possible to cross over to the other line as there were SS men everywhere, guns at the ready.

Friedel was directed to the young women. Older women and all women with children were put in a separate line. In this way four lines formed: approximately 150 young women and just as many young men; the other seven hundred were standing in their own lines on the side of the road.

Then the medical officer returned and called out to the elderly men, asking if there were any doctors among them. Four men leapt forward. The officer turned to Van der Kous, an elderly Amsterdam GP: 'What kind of diseases were there in the camp in Holland?'

Van der Kous hesitated and then told him something about eye diseases. Annoyed, the officer turned away.

Hans saw his opportunity: 'You probably mean contagious diseases. There were sporadic instances of scarlet fever, which followed a relatively benign course.'

'Any typhus?'

'No, not a single case.'

'Good. Back in line, all of you.' And then, turning to his adjutant: 'We'll take him.'

The adjutant beckoned Hans and took him to the end of the line of young men. He felt that he had escaped a great danger. And, sure enough, lorries had arrived in the meantime and the old men and women were being loaded on to them.

He saw now for the first time what it was really like under the SS, who began shoving, kicking and beating people. Many found it difficult to climb up on to the beds of the high lorries. But the *Sturmmänner*'s sticks guaranteed that all of them did their very best.

An elderly woman was bleeding badly from a blow to the head. A few people were left behind; they couldn't possibly get up on to the lorries and those who tried to come to their aid were chased away with a kick or a snarl.

The last lorry drove up and two SS men took an unfortunate old man by the arms and legs and threw him into the back. After that the women's line began to move. He had lost sight of Friedel, but knew she was there somewhere. When

11

the women were a couple of hundred metres away, the men started walking too.

The columns were heavily guarded. Soldiers were marching on both sides, guns at the ready. There was one guard for approximately every ten prisoners. Hans was fairly close to the end of the line. He saw the guards to his left and right signal each other. They looked around for a second, then the one on his left came up to Hans and asked him for his watch. It was beautiful and had a stopwatch. His mother had given it to him for his doctor's exam.

'I need it for my profession. I'm a doctor.'

A grin passed over the guard's face. '*Scheisse, Arzt*... A dog, that's what you are! Give me that watch!' The man grabbed him by the arm to pull it off. For an instant Hans tried to resist.

'Escape attempt, huh?' the man said, bringing up his rifle.

Hans realized how powerless he was and handed over the watch. He had no desire to be shot 'attempting to escape' on his first day in Auschwitz.

When they were crossing the railway track, he saw Friedel in the bend of the road. She waved and he sighed with relief. After the railway line they passed a barrier with sentry posts that seemed to mark the grounds of the camp proper. There were storage depots for building materials, sheds and enormous stacks of bricks and timber. There were small trains moved by manpower. Wagons, dragged by men. Here and there along the road were larger buildings, factories with the hum of machinery coming from the inside. And then more timber, bricks and sheds. A crane, lifting up cement buckets. There was building going on everywhere, and everywhere was alive. But more than cranes and small trains, one saw the men in their thieves' costumes. There was no motorization here; this was the work of thousands, of tens of thousands of hands.

Steam is practical; electricity is efficient, able to be put to work hundreds of kilometres away; petrol is fast and powerful. But people are cheap. That was clear from the hungry eyes. It was clear from the bare chests with ribs standing out like cords holding their bodies together. One saw it from the long lines of men carrying bricks, shuffling along in wooden clogs or, often enough, in bare feet. They trudged on without looking up or around. Their faces remained expressionless. No reaction to the new arrivals. Now and then a tractor pulling wagons full of bricks. The engine thumped slowly: oil engines. Hans couldn't help but think of the evenings he'd spent on the water, lying back on his boat and listening to the freighters chug by. What life had been like back then, the things it had promised him! He steeled himself. He felt that he couldn't start brooding now. He had to fight. Maybe he could make that old life come back one day.

Then they were standing in front of the gate and seeing the camp for the first time. It was made up of large, brick barracks. There were about twenty-five of them. They were two storeys high with pitched roofs and small attic windows. The streets between the buildings were well kept. There were pavements with tidy paving stones and small strips of lawn. Everything was clean, well painted and shining in the bright autumn sun.

It could have been a model village: a camp for thousands of labourers working on a great and useful project. Above the gate, in cast iron, the concentration camp slogan. Suggestive but dangerous: 'ARBEIT MACHT FREI'. A suggestion that was intended to calm the unending multitudes who entered here. Here and through many similar gates in other parts of Germany. But it was only an illusion, because this gate was a gate to hell and instead of 'Work sets you free' it should have said 'Abandon all hope, ye who enter here.'

Because the camp was surrounded by electric fences. Two rows of concrete posts, neatly whitewashed, three metres high. Barbed wire on the insulators. The wire looked strong, hard to get through. But what was even worse was invisible: 3,000 volts! With nothing but little red lamps glowing here and there to show that the electricity was on. And every ten metres a sign mounted on the fence with a skull and crossbones and the word 'stop' in German and Polish: *Halt, Stój*. Still, no barrier is sufficient unless every part of it can be kept under fire. That was why small watchtowers had been built every hundred metres, manned by SS guards with machine guns.

No, there was no way out of this place, unless by a miracle. The people they encountered in the camp said the same thing, because now that they were inside the wire, they were much less strictly guarded; the SS men had mostly handed over the task to prisoners. Prisoners, to be sure, who looked very different from the thousands at work outside the camp. These ones were wearing striped linen uniforms that were cleaner and well-fitting. Often they were dressed almost elegantly, with black hats and tall boots. On their left arms they wore red bands with numbers on them.

These were the *Blockälteste*, the heads of the various buildings, who organized everything in their block, running their own administration with the help of a clerk and distributing the food. They themselves did not go without; you could tell from their moon-shaped faces. They were all Poles and Reich Germans.*

But there were also a few Dutch prisoners around. The SS and the Blockälteste kept them at a distance because the newcomers still had all kinds of valuables on them. Nonetheless a few managed to come forward. They asked for watches and cigarettes: 'You're going to lose it all anyway.' But most of the new arrivals still didn't believe it and kept everything in their pockets. Hans gave a Dutchman a packet of cigarettes, but an SS man was watching and hit him. The Dutchman had already run off; he'd seen it coming in time.

A man appeared, small but with a Herculean build. He was apparently held in great respect.

'So, lads, when did you leave Westerbork?'

'Three days ago.'

'Any news?'

'Do you already know about the landing in Italy?'

'Of course, we read the paper. How are things in Holland?'

What could they say to that? They were more interested in hearing how things were here in Auschwitz, what their future would be.

'Who are you?' asked one of the newcomers.

'Leen Sanders, the boxer. I've been here a year.'

The newcomers were momentarily reassured. So it was possible to live here.

'Are there still a lot of people from your transport here?' asked Hans, who was already growing sceptical.

* A citizen of the German Reich. Under the Nazis' Nuremberg race laws, this status was reserved for 'racially pure' Germans.

'Don't ask too many questions. You'll see,' the boxer answered. 'Keep your eyes and ears open and your mouth shut.'

'But you look fine.'

Leen gave a wise smile. 'That's a boxer for you.'

'What will we have to do here?'

'You'll be assigned to the *Kommandos* that work outside the camp.'

Again Hans saw the people outside before him, those work-machines, lines of them carrying bricks and cement, their expressionless faces, dead eyes and emaciated bodies.

'What happens to the old people they took away in lorries?'

'Haven't you ever listened to the BBC?' Leen asked.

'I have.'

'Well, then you should know.'

Then Hans knew everything. He thought of Friedel, whose line he had lost sight of. He thought of his mother, his brother, of everyone he had seen leaving for Auschwitz. He thought of his studies, his practice, his ambitions. He thought once again of Friedel and their plans for the future. They were the thoughts of someone who was convinced he was going to die.

And yet, doubts were already appearing. Maybe he would be lucky, maybe. He was a doctor – no, he didn't dare hope, but he had to. He couldn't believe that he would die here, but he couldn't believe in life any more either.

A snarl brought him back to his senses. '*Aufgehen!*' They walked down Lagerstrasse between the big blocks. There were a lot of people out on the streets. Glass plates were mounted over the doors of some of the blocks:

Häftlingskrankenbau
Interne Abteilung
Eintritt verboten

Sitting in front of the hospital door were men in white suits with red stripes on the backs of their coats and along the seams of their trousers. They looked fit and healthy and must have been the doctors. These men hardly glanced at the new arrivals, but Hans saw that their lack of interest wasn't the same as the indifference of the thousands outside. With all those work slaves it had been the exhaustion, the deep despondency, that had prevented any mental effort. With these handsome men it was a kind of arrogance. After all, they were privileged, the camp 'prominents'. And what were they, the newcomers? Everyone was free to abuse and ridicule them.

They arrived at Block 26, the *Effektenkammer*. Leen explained what that meant. It was here that the prisoners' personal effects, clothes and other valuables, were stored. Above the windows you could see long lines of paper bags, each containing the property of one man. If somebody was going to be released from the camp, he'd get it all back.

Their clothes would not be stored. Jews were never released. There weren't any legal proceedings involving them. As they hadn't been sentenced to any punishment, they couldn't be freed.

Sure enough, between Blocks 26 and 27 they were ordered to undress. All of their clothes and everything they had on them was loaded on to a wagon. They were only allowed to keep a leather belt and a handkerchief. Hans tried to hold on to a few of his best instruments, but they were on to him in no time. A scrawny man with a band on his left arm – '*Lagerfriseur*' – was checking everyone. Those who had tried to keep something back had to surrender it after all and got a blow for good measure. Hans asked if he could keep his instruments. The man grinned and pocketed the lot.

There they stood. Now they had lost everything. The process had been slow, but now it was complete. Had not Schmidt, the Commissioner-General for Public Security in the Netherlands and Rauter's* representative for Jewish affairs, once said, 'The Jews will return to the land they came from, as naked as when they arrived here'?

Schmidt had not gone into detail about when those Jews had come, in the sixteenth and seventeenth centuries, and that they hadn't really arrived naked, but had often brought great treasures with them from the countries that had expelled them. Nor did he mention the historic rights of Dutch Jews, granted to them long ago by decree of William of Orange.

But how could he have spoken of the work of a Dutch hero who had fought for freedom? You couldn't expect that from heroes of Nazi oppression, who would not die with a patriotic prayer on their lips, but take to their heels to try to save their own skin.

Hans consoled himself with that thought. There was no doubt that he was in a bad position, but still: his fate was dark, *theirs* was certain. They would definitely fall and then, of all their victories, only one would be left: their victory over the Jews. Slowly but surely the Dutch Jews had been pushed towards their ruin.

* Hans Albin Rauter was the highest-ranking SS and Police Leader in the occupied Netherlands.

1940 All Jews sacked from public office.

1941 Banned from practising liberal professions, banned from using public transport, banned from shopkeeping, banned from theatres and parks, sport and everything that makes life beautiful; permitted capital capped at 10,000 guilders, later 250 guilders.

1942 Start of deportation, the ban on life itself.

Slowly, because the Dutch would not have tolerated 'their' Jews being exterminated at a time when the terror in Holland still hadn't taken hold.

NOW THEY WERE STANDING stark-naked in the burning sun, which beat down on their bodies for hours while the rituals to turn them into *Häftlinge* were completed.

Standing behind a long bench were six barbers, who cut off their hair and shaved their heads and bodies. They didn't ask if Sir would care for some powder or a scalp massage. They were rough, annoyed at having so much work to do on a hot afternoon. With their blunt razors they tore out the hair more than shaving it off, and they manhandled and sometimes hit anybody who didn't turn and twist enough to let them get everywhere easily. When the barber had finished, you got a note with a number to take to the tattooist. Hans got 150822.

He just smiled scornfully as the number was jabbed into the skin of his arm. Now he was no longer Dr van Dam, he was Häftling no. 150822. What did he care, as long as he could one day become Dr van Dam again? If he could only become Dr van Dam again.

And then that thought was there again, rolling back and forth in his head like an enormous ball and making a sound like a gramophone spinning out of control. Until a thump from behind brought him back to his senses.

They went into the washroom about fifty at a time. Inside were rows of showers next to each other. Three men had to share each shower, which gave a trickle of lukewarm water: too cold to soak off the dust and summer sweat, too hot to freshen up. Then a man wearing big rubber gloves came and smeared stinking disinfectant under their arms and over their pubic area with a single swipe.

After they had been sprayed with a Flit gun,* they were *rein*, which was a far cry from what we would call 'clean'. They were still half wet and sticky from sweat and disinfectant. Their skin was burning and the nicks and scrapes from being shaved smarted, but at least they were free of lice and fleas.

It was not easy to quickly find something that fitted in the large piles of clothing. The corridor of the *Bekleidungskammer*, as Block 27 was called, was dark when you came in from the bright sunlight and you had no idea what to actually take. You were pushed, shoved and yelled at, and if that didn't make you go fast enough, they hit you until you had gathered up some clothes. A vest, a coat and a pair of linen trousers, a hat and a pair of wooden shoes or sandals. They weren't given enough time to find the right sizes and looked like clowns in their convict uniforms.

One man's calves were showing; another was stumbling over his trousers. One was missing one of his coat sleeves; another had to roll his up. But all of the clothes had one thing in common – they were all equally dirty and patched, cobbled together from pieces of blue-and-white-striped material.

Now dressed, they were standing in front of the block again. The day was almost over, but the heat of late summer was still weighing heavily on the camp. They were hungry and thirsty, but no one was brave enough to ask for anything. They waited for another hour in Birkenallee, the street that ran

* Brand name of a hand-pumped insecticide spray used widely between 1928 and the mid-1950s.

behind the blocks: sitting on the edges of the pavement and on the benches by the strips of lawn, or simply lying stretched out on the street, exhausted and overcome by the misery they had been plunged into.

Registration tables had been set up in the street. All conceivable facts, personal or otherwise, were noted down: professional and other characteristics, particularly diseases – tuberculosis, venereal diseases – and once again the familiar questions about nationality and the number of Jewish grandparents.

Hans was talking to Eli Polak, a fellow doctor. Eli was a broken man. He had seen his wife when the lorries were at the train. She had fainted and they had thrown her on to the back of a lorry, followed by their child.

'I'll never see them again.'

Hans felt incapable of consoling him. He couldn't lie. 'You don't know that,' he answered, but with little conviction.

'Have you heard what happens in Birkenau?'

'What's Birkenau?' Hans asked.

'Birkenau is an enormous camp,' Eli answered. 'It's part of the whole Auschwitz complex. On arrival they tell all the old people and all the children they have to shower and take them into a big room. In reality, they gas them. Then they burn the bodies.'

'But it won't be like that with all of them,' Hans said, forcing himself to comfort him.

Then the soup arrived. Three kettles. Everyone was supposed to get one litre. They queued up in a long line. A few of the pushiest helped dole it out. They ate from large metal bowls, dented, with bare patches in the enamel. As there weren't enough bowls to go round, they put two litres in each bowl and you had to share it with someone. There were also spoons. About twenty. Those who didn't get a spoon had to drink from the bowl. That wasn't difficult. The soup was only thin. It had the odd hard bit floating in it and there were discussions as to whether they were beech or elm leaves. But none of that mattered. Most of them were still well nourished, and then it doesn't make much difference whether you get a litre of hot water or a litre of food in your stomach.

Suddenly they were being hurried up: 'Quick, it's almost roll call!' They slurped down the hot soup as fast as they could and were taken to a large wooden warehouse that had been built between two blocks. It was a laundry. In one half, clothes were being washed in big cauldrons; in the other there were showers. Hans counted one hundred and forty-four. Along the walls were benches where people could get undressed. They sat on the benches and waited.

They heard that after the roll call, which was held outside at that time, they would be travelling on to Buna. The man from the administration who told them was bombarded with questions: 'What is that, Buna?' 'Is it good there?' 'Do you get soup like this there too?'

He said it was all right. You had to work in a synthetic rubber factory. The food was good there because you were in the service of an industrial concern. The man gave a knowing smile.

Hans discovered a Belgian.

'Have you been here long?'

'A year.'

'Is it possible to stick it out?'

'Sometimes. If you're lucky and get into a good Kommando.'

'What's a good Kommando?'

'The laundry or the hospital or something like that. Almost all of the Kommandos that stay in the camp in the daytime are good. The food Kommandos too. But as a Jew you don't stand a chance of them.'

'I'm a doctor. Could I get into the hospital?'

'Didn't you tell them you were a doctor?'

'Yes, but they brushed me off. Where do they take the women?'

'The women from this transport were brought into the camp. There's a women's block here where they do all kinds of experiments.' Hans's heart stood still. Friedel, here in this camp. Experiments! What could that mean?

He told the Belgian about Friedel and asked him if he would take a message to her, as he himself would be leaving for Buna. The Belgian said it was extremely difficult because it was very dangerous to go near the women's block.* Just then an SS man came in. They all jumped up, as they had been taught. He asked the big question: 'Are there any doctors here?'

Three of them leapt forward: Hans, Eli Polak and a young fellow they didn't know.

The SS man asked how long they had been practising medicine. The young chap turned out to be a junior doctor. Eli had been a GP for eight years. The SS man sent Eli back to the others: 'You're going to Buna with them.' He took Hans and the younger man away with him.

---

* Many notes were exchanged between women in Block 10 and their husbands. Eddy himself was often able to enter Block 10, bringing soup, for example, and men were able to smuggle notes and letters, and food packages, in and out. There was a severe risk involved.

They walked through the camp, past all the buildings, and arrived at Block 28, where they had to wait in the corridor. It was a long, concrete corridor with whitewashed walls and doors on both sides. On the doors were signs: *Ambulanz*, *Schreibstube*, *Operationssaal*, *Hals-Nasen-Ohrenarzt*, *Röntgenraum* and many others. Halfway along the corridor were concrete stairs up to the first floor.

After a couple of minutes, a man in a white suit arrived. He took them to the end of the corridor. *Aufnahme* was written on the frosted-glass door. It was a large room, more like a ward, and only half filled with bunks. In the other half there were a few benches, scales and a large table covered with books and documents. This was where everyone who was admitted to the hospital registered, either as a patient or a member of staff.

They were met by a small fat Pole. He snarled at them, wanting to know why they looked so filthy, told them to get completely undressed and pointed out a bed. The beds were triple bunks. Hans lay naked under two thin blankets on the top bunk. He tried to roll himself up a little in the blankets because the straw in the mattress itched.

Just after he had lain down, a man clambered up to his bed. He was about thirty, with a round face and a pair of glasses perched jauntily on his nose.

'What's your name?' he asked. 'Are you a doctor?'

'Yes, I'm Van Dam. And you?'

'De Hond. I've been here for three weeks now. I saw the *Lagerarzt* last week. He took me on and now I'm on the *Pfleger* reserve list.'

'Where did you study?' Hans asked.

'In Utrecht. I was at the children's hospital.'

'What kind of work do you do here?'

'Oh, all kinds. They come and get you for all sorts of odd jobs all day long. You'll see. It's filthy work, with cadavers and so on. Don't you have any clothes?'

No, Hans didn't have any. They would need to be organized the next day. De Hond would help him.

'Do you know anything about the women's block here?'

'Oh,' De Hond replied, clearly nervous. 'Yes, that's Block 10; my wife's there. She's a doctor as well. She arrived there three weeks ago.'

Hans was glad to hear there was a Dutch doctor there. He told De Hond about Friedel and that she too had been taken to Block 10.

'Hmm,' said De Hond. 'We'll have to see what can be done for her.'

'What do you mean?'

'Well, Samuel, the professor who works there, promised me he won't take my wife because she's a doctor. Maybe he'll be willing to bend the rules for a doctor's wife too.'

'What do they do with those women?'

'You'll have to ask Samuel that yourself. He comes here every day.'

'Can I see my wife?'

'That's very difficult. If they catch you, they'll put you in the *Bunkier*, in the prison, and then you can count yourself lucky if you get off with twenty-five.'

'What do you mean, twenty-five?'

'That's the standard punishment. Twenty-five strokes on the backside.'

Hans smiled. Things like that didn't scare him. You just had to make sure they didn't catch you. And anyway, it would be worth it to see Friedel. De Hond promised to take him with him the next evening. Then it was nine o'clock and lights off.

But it wasn't dark in the ward. Block 28 was the last block in the row and admissions was on the side, near the fence. The lights along the wire were on and there were brighter lights on every second concrete post. Anything that came near the wire would be well lit.

It was an impressive sight, those long lines of bright lights with red warning lights between them. They shone into the room, illuminating the patients, who had been allocated beds in admissions before being presented to the Lagerarzt the next day. Hans didn't want to see the light any more; it frightened him. He closed his eyes, but kept opening them again for another look, as if forcing himself to take in the painful reality. He grew nervous and turned from side to side, but the light pursued him. He pulled the blankets up over his head, but couldn't block it out – it shone through everywhere. There was no escaping it: he was in a *Konzentrationslager*. Whether you turned your head away or shrank back under the blankets, that awareness remained. No matter what you tried to think, that thought dominated everything, just as the lights on the wire followed you wherever you looked.

Hans wept. He wasn't crying out of anger, like he had as a boy when he hadn't got his way about something. This was a quiet weeping that seemed to rise up by itself. There was no storm inside him. He was simply overflowing with sorrow, and the tears flowed automatically. But fortunately he was tired, dead tired. He didn't even wipe away his tears. He no longer felt that he was crying and slowly the flame of his consciousness went out.

In concentration camps people experience many happy hours every day. The lights are turned off for them, the electric current is shut down and the wire is cut. The soul can free itself from the exhausted and tormented body. In the realm the Häftling enters at night, there are no SS men, no Blockälteste and no *Kapos*. There is only one master: the great longing. There is only one law: freedom.

Life is a cycle made up of two periods: from the morning gong to the night gong, and from the night gong to the morning gong. When the morning gong sounds, the senses come to life and the soul is enchained: paradise is over.

HALF AN HOUR AFTER the gong, the patients began arriving. Hans was able to watch the whole process from his bed.

The men undressed outside, tied their clothes up in a bundle with the number on the jacket visible on top, then entered the block naked. In the washroom they were all washed and their numbers were written on their chests to make sure the Lagerarzt didn't waste any of his valuable time checking who was who.

From the washroom they went back to admissions, where they were registered and could start waiting. There were approximately sixty of them. They were all washed and registered by seven, but the Lagerarzt didn't arrive until about ten. Still, nobody was bored. Most of the men were glad to be able to stay away from work for a day. Many were too ill to be bored. They were able to sit on the few benches and otherwise nobody paid any attention to them. A number of them were in pain or running a fever, but nobody was allowed to give them anything or help them until they had seen the Lagerarzt.

At nine thirty Hans and Van Lier, the junior doctor, had to get up. They too were going to be presented to the Lagerarzt. It was a strange way to appear before your future boss but, on the other hand, it was perhaps better to be introduced naked than in one of those filthy uniforms. Then the call sounded in the corridor: '*Arztvormelder, antreten!*'

The Reich Germans went first. They were prisoners too but, in this camp, with mostly Polish and Jewish inmates, they occupied a special position. After the Germans, the Poles and other 'Aryans'. The Jews came last.

They went through the corridor, all trotting in line to out-patients, which turned out to be in quite good state. Running through the middle of the room was a metal bar at about knee height, which the patients had to stand behind. Generally, nurses stood on the other side in front of large tables with wound-dressing materials while the clerks sat behind a glass wall in the office, where all those who had ever visited the outpatients clinic were listed in a card-index system.

This time there were no patients and no nurses, only the Lagerarzt with another member of the SS, an *Unterscharführer*, and two Polish prisoners – the Polish *Lagerältester*, who was responsible for all prisoner doctors, and the admissions doctor. The Poles had examined all those who had to see the SS doctor the previous evening, and were there to present them to him now.

Not that the presentations amounted to much: there were no explanations, no discussions, no further examinations. Quick, quick, the *Obersturmführer* didn't have any time, he never had any time. A diagnosis read off a card, a fleeting glance at the patient and he was ready with his answer: admission or *Blockschonung*. In the latter case, the sick prisoner received an exemption from work for a certain number of days and could stay in the barracks. This was for those who didn't need to be admitted to hospital but still couldn't work, due to things like injuries to their fingers or boils on their legs.

The sick Jews, however, usually needed to be admitted, because their general condition was extremely poor. These were the people who worked in the harshest Kommandos, never received packages and were always cheated the most when the Blockälteste were distributing food in the barracks.

Admission, admission, Blockschonung, admission. They got through the whole line in a few minutes and only the two Dutchmen were left.

'Doctors, arrived on transport yesterday,' the Polish doctor reported.

The Lagerarzt nodded: 'Assign!'

Then it was done. They raced back to the admissions ward and had to get back into bed. Hans was happy. After all, this was his chance. Life in the hospital would be very different from outside on those building sites. Nurses took the patients who had been admitted to the various blocks: surgery, internal diseases, infectious diseases. The others went outside to get dressed. Those who had Blockschonung were given a note for their block clerk.

De Hond came to fetch the two Dutchmen and took them outside. The clothes of the people who had been admitted to hospital were still lying there. A few nurses were already untying the bundles and removing anything of value from the pockets. Any clothes that were good and intact were laid to one side. The rest went on a barrow, from which the two young men were allowed to pick something out.

Afterwards they were somewhat bearably dressed. They even had leather shoes – very down-at-heel, true, but easier on the feet than wooden sandals. But now that they were dressed, they could also work, and were immediately claimed for a job. They had to take the barrow of clothes to disinfection.

The Kapo from disinfection was standing at the door. He was the absolute ruler over the twelve men who worked in his wooden outbuilding. When the two novices approached, he gave a sarcastic bow.

'Two grand gentlemen. And where are the gentlemen from?'

Van Lier tried to be polite: 'We come from Holland, Sir.'

The Kapo laughed: 'Then you'll soon be dead. The Dutch all drop dead here in a couple of weeks. You're too delicate. You can't work.'

Hans shrugged as if to say, *We'll see*. Just then the big steam boiler opened and the trolley with disinfected clothes came rolling out.

'Go on. Unload it.'

They unloaded it. It was hot, terribly hot: the clothes were still at boiling point. Steam was billowing up everywhere. They burnt their hands and choked in the scalding air. Within seconds they were dripping with sweat. But the Kapo kept harassing them and when they stopped to gasp for air, he shoved them and snarled, 'Faster, you idiots!'

After they'd pulled all of the clothes out of the boiler, Hans was reeling as he tried to catch his breath in front of the small building. Suddenly someone gave him a friendly pat on the shoulder. It was a Polish Jew, one of the lads working in disinfection.

'Our Kapo's a sterling fellow, isn't he?'

Hans gave him an uncomprehending look.

'Well, he was joking with you, but you don't know what the Lager really means.'

'Have you been here long then?'

The Pole pointed at the number on his chest: 62,000-something. 'I've been here one and a half years now. I went through the hard times. Now it's like a sanatorium. They hardly ever hit you and if you don't turn into a *Mussulman*, you're in no danger at all.'

'What do you mean? What's a Mussulman?'

'You really are new, aren't you? Have you heard of those people who go to Mecca on pilgrimage? Emaciated, completely starved, skin and bones, characters like Gandhi? They're Mussulmen.'

Hans didn't understand. 'What do they do with them?'

'They can't work any more. They go to the crematorium. It used to be different. I was working in Birkenau. Back then, when the Kommandos turned out and the Kapo reported, "Roadworks Kommando, 270 men," the SS at the gate said, "That's forty too many." Then the SS guard who was leading the Kommando and the Kapos would make sure to beat forty men to death that day. Marching back that night, we'd smell our mates who had been superfluous in the morning roasting. They didn't care if they were Mussulmen or not. Thousands died like that and anyone who was lucky enough to come through it croaked some other way. Picture it: eight kilometres out in the morning and eight back at night. Standing in water all day scooping up gravel, sometimes up to your ankles, sometimes up to your waist. In winter we'd often come back with clothes frozen solid and as hard as a plank. And the beatings! Don't think you could lean on your shovel, not for a second. There'd be an SS man there right away who knew what to do with you. Look.' He showed Hans his leg: a big scar. And his left hand: two fingers missing.

'Smashed to a pulp. My mate was smoking a cigarette on the job. I asked him for a drag. Just when he was about to pass me the cigarette, the guard came. He swung at me with the butt of his rifle. I deflected it and my hand got caught between the rifle butt and a wall. There was a second blow for my friend. That evening we carried him back to the camp unconscious. We might have been able to save him, but it was a long roll call that night. A good three hours, and he had to lie there all that time.'

'Couldn't you get him any help?'

'It was roll call and the number had to be right. No matter what state you were in, you had to be counted.'

Jacques, the Polish Jew, was quiet for a moment, staring at the stumps on his left hand. Hans looked around and was suddenly shocked. Diagonally across from disinfection there was a block with wire mesh on the windows, and behind that wire he could see women. Yes, there was a sign too: Block 10. So this was the women's block.

Jacques saw the surprise on his face. 'What do you see?'

Hans hesitated. 'I think that's where my wife is.'

Jacques could hardly believe it. 'Your wife arrived yesterday too? Man, you really are a lucky dog.'

'Could I see her?'

'In the evening. It's risky. You have to be prepared for that.'

The Pfleger who had accompanied them with the clothes came over: 'Back to the block.'

The rest of the day passed with bustling inactivity. There was always a loose straw to be found on one of the beds. There was always a window with a smudge on it. Grab a piece of scrap paper and clean it. It was boring, but Hans didn't complain. Instead he thought of the work machines outside. Every day you put behind you unscathed in here was one day closer to the end.

34

That was what Kalker said too. Kalker was a doctor from The Hague. Hans had seen him now and then at the home of relatives who had him as their GP. Now he was working in Block 21, the surgical block. He had dropped by to see which new Dutchmen had arrived. 'It's a rude awakening, all right,' he told Hans and Van Lier. 'Not what we expected.'

'How long have you been here?'

'Three weeks now. I was here in admissions for the first fortnight, then they assigned me to Block 21.'

'Do you assist the surgeons?'

Kalker burst out laughing: 'Yes, after studying the anatomical topography of the lavatory construction, I've moved on to cleaning work. You have no idea how complicated and fascinating it is. You mop the floors four times a day and scrub the toilet bowls with sand every other day. My lavatories are a feast for the eyes. I have two: one for patients, with twelve bowls in two rows, and one with a row of six for staff. In the small lavatory there is a closed-off cubicle for the camp's leading lights – the *Blockältester* and the Lagerältester – and rumour has it that it's sometimes even used by the Lagerarzt. But that honour hasn't been granted me just yet. In any case he's only in the camp for half an hour each day, and I'm sure he's quite capable of holding it in for that long. It would really be too much for him to have to sit down on a toilet that Häftlinge have sat on beforehand.'

Hans was enjoying the cheerful tone Kalker had adopted for his story. 'Do you get enough to eat?' he asked.

'Well, it's all right. There's usually seconds of the soup, so I get one and a half litres. And once you've been officially assigned somewhere, you get extra bread twice a week.'

'How much exactly?' Van Lier asked.

'You get one litre of soup a day and a ration of bread, then, twice a week, forty grams of margarine, a spoonful of jam and a forty-gram slice of sausage. But don't expect too much. The margarine is only fifteen per cent fat – the rest is synthetic thickener – and the sausage is only fifty per cent meat – soggy horsemeat.'

'How much nutritional value, how many calories, is that altogether?'

'I've more or less worked it out,' Kalker said. 'The soup's not worth much, about 150 to 200 calories a litre. Altogether you manage about 1,500 calories a day. Of course, that's not enough. Even at rest the body needs 1,600. It's clear that someone who has to do hard labour here soon turns into a Mussulman.'

'But if you see those Pfleger, they all look fine,' Hans objected.

'Sure, but first, they're mostly Poles, who get packages from home, and second, they're often the biggest "organizers" – or, to not mince words, thieves. The Pfleger dish out the soup. The patients get the liquid on the top; that way the few potatoes and beans the soup contains are left over for the Pfleger.'

Just then a tall man came in. He was older, definitely over sixty. He had a slight stoop and was wearing an old-fashioned pince-nez on his nose.

De Hond leapt up. 'Good afternoon, Professor.'

Hans realized that this must be Professor Samuel. He introduced himself and waited to see how the conversation developed. The standard questions: when had they arrived, political news, etc. Hans told him about the transport and their arrival in Auschwitz, placing the emphasis on Friedel.

The professor took the bait. 'In point of fact, I have spoken to several of those new Dutchwomen. I don't recall the name Van Dam though. You should try to speak to your wife at the window, but be careful. I'll give her your regards.'

Hans wanted to ask the professor to deliver a letter for him, but restrained himself. He was counting on the professor for more important favours. 'Do you visit the women's block often?'

'Every day. I work there.'

Hans feigned ignorance. 'Are you the attending physician?'

'Not entirely. I have certain tasks to fulfil. In a sense, those women are study material.'

'Isn't that unpleasant for them?'

The professor became defensive. 'There are certain experiments that are highly unpleasant, perhaps even deleterious for the women concerned, but what I do is very different. I have managed to interest the SS in research into the development of uterine cancer. I have access to a great number of women for that purpose and as a result they are not used for other, *unpleasant*, experiments.'

Hans gave a nod of understanding. He was more than a little sceptical about the professor's good intentions, but didn't want it to show. He still needed the professor's help.

'Decide for yourself,' Samuel continued. 'With my women, I remove a small piece of mucous membrane from the cervix. That sample is then studied under a microscope. Among a certain proportion of the women, we find particular abnormalities in the tissue. We see cells whose structure deviates greatly from the norm. I believe that these cells later give rise to cancer. In this way I hope to identify the cause of tumour formation.'

Judging by the professor's account, the tests were not very harmful to the women. Hans just didn't understand what particular purpose they had. Japanese researchers had already rubbed the skin of white mice with tar products and meticulously tracked the resulting changes to the tissue. Their experiment had resulted in the formation of artificial cancers, establishing that the tar contained carcinogenic substances. At the same time, general medical practice had already shown the medical profession something analogous: lip and tongue cancers in habitual pipe-smokers. Once people had thought these cancers were caused by sucking; now they realized that the true cause was the tar products that formed in the stem of the pipe.

It seemed to Hans that, whether the tests were useful or not, it was still improper to use people for vivisection against their will. He had to reserve judgement though, as he didn't have enough facts yet and, in any case, he had other things on his mind.

'Will the Dutchwomen who have just arrived also be subjected to the experiments?'

'Undoubtedly,' Samuel replied. 'But I can help your wife. I'll put her on my list. That way she won't fall into the hands of the others and I'll be able to keep her out of harm's way for as long as possible.'

Hans thanked the professor. He was a little relieved. He didn't know what the promise was worth, but he had achieved something. For the time being, Friedel would be spared.

I T WAS EVENING. THE lights on the wire had been turned on. The *Stubenältester*, a fat Pfleger, appeared. He called to the two newcomers: 'Corpse Kommando.'

De Hond grinned. 'That's a nice job. Roll up your sleeves for the gunge.'

They went outside, where there was a large lorry with a zinc-covered bed. The corpse carriers were bringing the dead bodies up from the cellar. Two per stretcher. They could easily carry two at once because, by the time they died, these emaciated wretches who had been worked into the ground were already skeletons, just skin and bones.

The corpse carriers took the bodies one at a time by the arms and legs and tossed them up on to the back of the lorry, where Hans and Van Lier had to stack them. When the cadavers landed, they slid to the front of the bed under their own momentum as the zinc was soon slippery from the fluid leaking out of them; Hans and Van Lier had to jump out of the way to try to keep their clothes clean. Once a body had stopped sliding, they picked it up and laid it neatly on the pile, then quickly jumped out of the way again because the next one would be already sliding towards them. With the corpse carriers doing their best to hit Hans and Van Lier with the bodies, the Dutchmen were constantly dancing back and forth on the back of the lorry. It was a gruesome affair.

It was now almost dark and they were lit by the lights on the wire. The cadavers kept sliding over the bed towards the two dancing men, whose hands were now so filthy and slippery they could hardly hold the bodies any more and definitely couldn't stop them from rubbing against their clothes.

By the time Hans made it back to admissions, he felt unbelievably filthy. There was only cold water to wash his hands in. He didn't have any soap and no one would lend him any. As far as washing his clothes went, that was completely out of the question.

Beautiful slogans about the virtues of cleanliness were painted on the walls of the washroom: '*Reinlichkeit ist der Weg zur Gesundheit*', '*Halte dich sauber*' and similar noble sentiments. That was what it was like with the Germans; the slogan had to replace reality, and if you repeated a motto often enough and stuck it on all the walls, everyone would end up believing it. '*Wir fahren gegen Engeland*', '*V = Victory*', '*Die Juden sind unser Unglück*'.

The Tibetans have paper wheels with prayers written on them. The wheels turn in the wind so the prayer is repeated over and over again. If you had been in the washroom and rinsed yourself off with cold water, you just had to read '*Halte dich sauber*' three times and everything was healthy again. Hans would have rather been amongst the Tibetans. As far as civilization went, the only lead the Germans had on them was in their murder techniques.

When he got back to admissions, De Hond was looking for him. 'Come on, Van Dam, it's almost dark. We're going to Block 10.'

They went out into Birkenallee. There were quite a lot of people there, strolling aimlessly to and fro. A few men were standing near Block 10. De Hond led Hans over and introduced him to one of them: 'Adriaans, a fellow doctor.'

Adriaans couldn't stop asking questions about Westerbork and his parents-in-law, but Hans found it almost impossible to pay attention. He couldn't take his eyes off the barred windows ten metres away, where female faces kept appearing every now and then.

Adriaans continued. He had been here for a couple of months already – he had been so lucky. His wife Ima was in this block. She was working as a nurse and he was at the Hygienic Institute – to be precise, the *Hygienisch-bakteriologischen Untersuchungsstelle der Waffen-SS und Polizei Südost*. That was where the laboratory research for all the camps in the whole area was carried out. It was fairly normal work. The SS lab assistants rushed you, but – and then, without turning, he said, 'Hello, Ima. Hello, darling, how was it today?'

A young woman had appeared at the window closest to Birkenallee. She was wearing a white shirt and had a red scarf around her head. She gave a scarcely audible reply.

Then Hans couldn't take it any more. He called out to Ima, asking her if she would look for Friedel. But the lads gave him a thump and made it clear that he had to be quiet. The corner of the camp was fifty metres away at most. There – on the other side of the first fence – the sentry was at his post on his watchtower. One loud word called out to a woman; a shot; and the idyll would be over for ever.

Waiting had never been Hans's greatest talent. But now it was as if he had been waiting for years and could no longer bear the tension. The atmosphere was loaded. It was twilight and women appeared at the windows like silhouettes in a shadow theatre. It was a sultry, late-summer evening and the air was full of mystery. As if in a tale from the *Thousand and One Nights*, the young men stood here outside this enormous harem, full of longing for the women who were rightfully theirs.

And then her voice came, like a song from a distant minaret reaching him through a quiet Oriental night, a dream of longing and wistfulness. As gentle as the whispering of hidden lovers and as sad as the song of the imam, calling to the Prophet, with his body bent low to the ground.

'Hans, sweetheart. Thank God you're here too.'

'Friedel, now we're together, it makes all the difference.'

He tried to pick her out, but the growing darkness had made the women braver and they were now crowded up to the windows, all looking alike in their red headscarves. He told her so.

'I'll take my scarf off so you can see how beautiful I am now.'

There, at the second window, that was her, his girl. He smiled. Of course she was beautiful. He would always find her equally beautiful, whether she had hair or whether her head was shaven, and, if he could possess her again, she would be the same for him no matter how violated.

'What's it like in your block?' The lads had taken position in front of Hans so the sentry couldn't see him and now he could speak a little more freely.

'Oh, it's not bad here. You don't have to work and it's clean.'

'Friedel, I've spoken to the professor. You needn't be afraid. He says that as a doctor's wife he'll spare you.'

'Good. Apparently some awful things go on here.'

Hans saw the woman next to Friedel nudge her. Clearly that was something you weren't allowed to talk about.

'Friedel, dear, I'm in the hospital, I'll be able to stick it out there ...'

Then it was over. He heard a whistle and the lads gave Hans a push. They were walking along Birkenallee and no longer paying any attention to the women's block.

A young man came up to them. 'It was me who whistled. Claussen's in the camp.'

Claussen was the *Rapportführer*. He came into the camp at odd times so he could report back to the *Lagerführer* in the evenings about what was happening. He was a real German, tall and blond, who looked like he'd just stepped out of a picture. In the mornings he was mean, but in the evenings he was dangerous, because in the evenings he was usually drunk.

The urge to cruelty, which is systematically suppressed in every civilized person by their environment and education from early childhood, had been stirred in the German nation. National Socialist morality, plus the required dose of alcohol, turned men into devils – although that is actually an insult to the devil, because he is a just avenger. The devil only torments those who have earned their punishment, or when he, as with Faust, is justified by a contract and terms of sale. Nazis throw themselves on defenceless victims with no justification at all.

That was what happened that night with Claussen, the Rapportführer. The lads observed him from a safe distance. Everyone who came near him was in for it – a kick or a blow – and those who didn't make off in time were beaten to the ground and received a terrible introduction to Claussen's boots.

But up came Willy, the Lagerältester, the senior representative of the Häftlinge. Smiling, he approached Claussen, cap in hand. The object of fear hesitated a moment, but when he saw Willy's open expression and friendly nods, he calmed down. He gave the Lagerältester a jovial pat on the shoulder and went off with him, probably to have a drink together.

The camp could breathe again. Willy had saved the day. Willy was a decent chap. He felt duty-bound to take the side of the Häftlinge and wasn't scared of running risks to do so. He was a German, but as a Communist he'd already spent eight years in the *KZ*.

Dering, however, was different. Dering was the Lagerältester for the *Krankenbau*. Like all the *Älteste*, he had been chosen from among the prisoners by the SS. Hans first met him the next morning.

'What kind of doctor are you?'

Hans told him in just a few words. He felt an aversion to this man, who leant back in his chair with such indifference and addressed a fellow doctor as if he were a naughty boy.

'Enough. Wait in the corridor.'

Several Häftlinge were already waiting there. Most of them were young Poles, who were going to be presented to Dering as potential Pfleger. In addition, three Jews: Hans, the junior doctor Van Lier and an elderly man who introduced himself as Dr Benjamin, a paediatrician from Berlin. He was from the same transport as Hans, but after disinfection Professor Samuel had taken him straight to the hospital. He knew the professor from their student days.

After Dering had seen the last of the young Poles, a clerk came with a list. He put the Jewish doctors to one side and took away the Poles. After a few minutes he came back.

'You have to go into quarantine first,' he told them. 'Then you can be placed in the Krankenbau.'

When Hans had come back from seeing the Lagerarzt the previous day, he'd thought he'd achieved his goal, but De Hond had warned him: 'You've got past the German, but you've still got to get past the Pole.'

Unfortunately De Hond had been right. The Lagerarzt had taken him on, but the Polish head of the hospital had now fobbed him off with quarantine. Would he make it back into the hospital, or was this just a ploy on the part of the Lagerältester?

The possibility terrified Hans. Why weren't the young Poles going into quarantine with them? Why just the three Jews?

IN QUARANTINE HANS GOT to know Lager life. He had to share the top berth of a triple bunk with two others: the elderly Dr Benjamin and a Russian. In the morning at half past four the big gong on the roof of the kitchen was rung and within ten seconds an enormous racket had been unleashed. Everyone was awake and climbing down the bunks and then the *Stubenälteste* were climbing up to make sure nobody was still snoozing. If they were, they would be beaten out of bed.

They joined the long line waiting in the central corridor for a turn to wash. That hour spent waiting was a harsh ordeal for Hans. After waking up, he always had to go straight to the toilet; he had been like that his whole life. And now he had to stand in line wearing just a vest and with no opportunity to slip off for a minute. If you tried to seek sympathy from the Stubenältester or the guard at the door, you would only get a few slaps for your trouble.

That hour, too, came to an end. Then you were given a pair of wooden sandals at the door and went downstairs. That was where the latrines and the washroom were. At the latrines: the *Scheissmeister*, keeping a close watch to make sure nobody made a mess. He had a stick in his hand and knew how to use it. In the washroom: the *Bademeister*, again with a stick. Slogans on the walls: '*Sauberkeit ist der halbe Weg zur Gesundheit*' and similarly beautiful statements. Cleanliness might be halfway to health, but try getting clean when you only have a few drops of cold water, no soap and have to dry yourself with your vest. After washing there was an inspection and woe betide those who weren't clean!

Then, making the beds. Wherever they were, the Germans had a thing about these beds. In the first place they were not meant to be slept in, but looked at. And if the blankets were dirty or the straw mattress empty, or if a diseased person or a dead body had been lying in the bed, it didn't matter, as long as it was well made, without a crease in the blanket or a loose straw on top of it.

And then queuing up again, for a mouthful of coffee, in that interminable line behind the bunks with two hundred Poles and Russians. Whether you were thirsty or not, you had to line up. There were far too few bowls, so two of you drank out of one bowl and you had to be quick about it because others were already waiting for that bowl. '*Halte dich sauber*' was written on the walls – and they all drank out of the same bowl! Keep clean while slurping your coffee out of it and eating your soup out of it with a piece of wood as a spoon.

Hans couldn't help but think of the story about a parson visiting a farmer – one of his parishioners – and sitting at the table to eat groats out of a common pot. When he gets a lump in his mouth, the farmer notices and says, 'Spit it back in, parson. I just had it too.' What kind of things had been spat back into the bowls here?

Hans still had a humorous take on it all, but not Dr Benjamin. The old man was broken. He couldn't bear being hit and harried all day long and at the same time his helplessness meant he received more slaps than anyone. When they finally had their coffee, he of course couldn't drink it fast enough. He paid for it with a slap. After the coffee, the order: 'All on the beds.' It cost Dr Benjamin a kick.

After that, they spent a couple of hours sitting on the beds, while more privileged prisoners, the 'room orderlies', mopped the floor. Privileged because they earned an extra ladle of soup for it. Hans was bored; he just happened to be a very active person. But he thought of something Leen Sanders had said: 'Every day you're in quarantine is a bonus. Just as much to eat as in the work Kommandos, but no work.' You conserved energy, sure, but it turned you into a nervous wreck. Waiting for coffee, waiting for soup, waiting for blows and snarls.

Outside now and then in the daytime. It was good to be between the blocks, but the September sun turned the place into an oven in the afternoons. There was one good thing about going outside: Hans was in a room full of Poles and Russians he couldn't exchange a single word with; Dr Benjamin and he were the only Jews, and their fellow prisoners were hostile towards them. But outside you met people from the other quarantine rooms. There were Czechs and Austrians, and the most beautiful thing was that you could always find someone who was prepared to explain to you that the war could only last another three months at most.

And then, after three days, the great feast: a package from Friedel with a couple of slices of bread with jam and margarine. In quarantine they just broke the bread into pieces. This bread had been sliced neatly and made into a sandwich prepared by a woman's hand, his wife's.

She was so close, three hundred metres at most, but there were guards on the doors and if they caught him it would mean a real thrashing. It was a chance you could take, but it could also lead to a report to the SS and that would mean a punishment detail, which was something he couldn't risk. And so he lived with the tension of inactivity, waiting, bread and blows, boredom and longing.

After a week things changed.

It was hot between the blocks, very hot. A sliver of shade was hugging the side of Block 13 and only expanding slowly, because time passed slowly on that endless, scorching sunny day.

Crowded into that sliver was half of Central and Eastern Europe. The other half couldn't fit into the shade and was squatting against the sunlit wall of Block 12, or lying stretched out in the dust, pointing every which way. Sleeping with their hats on their faces, naked torsos filthy from a grimy mix of sweat and sand.

Hans preferred the heat of the sun to the body heat of the men crammed into the shade. He was strolling along with Oppenheim, who was giving an exposition on his favourite theme: the end of the war in relation to the petroleum shortage.

Then a loud voice: 'Everyone with wooden shoes fall in.' Hans hesitated. He was one of the few with shoes. All of the others had gone straight to quarantine from disinfection. They were still wearing sandals. His hesitation proved disastrous because the Blockältester, who had yelled the order, was right there. He dragged Hans along, spewing out curses, because he had seen him trying to slink off.

Altogether there were fifteen men, mostly Poles – coarse, sturdy young fellows, still well fed from home. They marched in twos to Block 1, where there were wagons. They were given straps that were wired to one of the wagons and had to use them to haul the wagon to the gate. The Blockältester, who was supervising them, announced: '*Häftling 27903 mit 15 Häftlingen zur Strassenbau.*'

So that was it: roadworks. The SS man noted the Kommando down in a book that lay on the counter of the *Blockführerstube*. Then they continued on their way.

Hans smiled when he thought of the day of his arrival, a week ago now. All that human machinery pulling wagons. Now he was pulling one himself, a small cog in one of those fifteen-cog machines, and if he didn't pull hard enough for a moment he would immediately get a kick from the Pole behind him.

'*Dalej, dalej!*' cried the Poles; '*Davai, bystro!*' the Russians; '*Los, Schweinehunde!*' the Blockältester, and if an SS man happened to be passing, he shouted it twice as hard and hit whoever was closest with his stick – on the back or on the head, it didn't matter where, as long as he demonstrated what an enthusiastic Blockältester he was.

It was like that everywhere with the Nazis. The SS yelled at everyone, including the Blockälteste, the Blockälteste yelled and lashed out – at the Poles too, and they in turn chose the weakest to yell at. The weakest were Hans and a Polish Jew called Leib.

They didn't say anything in reply. Hans could feel that the Poles were shouting to release the tension from being shouted at themselves. The Führer shouted at his generals. They could bear it because they in turn got to shout at their officers. And the officers shouted at the soldiers. Like a billiard ball that stops rolling when it hits another ball, the soldiers calmed down again after beating the prisoners and shouting at them.

The Blockältester hit the Poles and the Poles hit Hans. The Führer's blow had reached Hans, where it couldn't do any more harm because Hans was powerless.

He was also powerless when they arrived at the pile of gravel. They were meant to load the gravel in two gangs, but he was always the dupe because when it was time for the gang to be relieved there was never anyone to take his shovel. It made sense: 15 = 7+8. Eight of them worked and seven were there to relieve them, so the eighth didn't have anyone to relieve him and the eighth was always Hans. He complained to Leib, who said something to the others in Polish. They laughed, but nothing happened.

They dragged the wagon back and forth many times, picking up gravel outside and carting it back to the camp, where others from quarantine were already at work spreading it on the streets. Hans was wet through. His hands were blistered from the shovel and his feet were chafed where the edges of the wooden shoes scraped over his bare skin. After being pushed to the front so many times by the Poles, he went over to the SS guard next to the pile of gravel. But he didn't get a chance to complain; the mighty *Sturmmann* did not wish to be disturbed. Hans took the slap in the face with gritted teeth and the work carried on as before, with shoves from the Blockältester and mocking from the Poles.

When they entered the camp after the sixth trip with the fully loaded wagon, all of the other Kommandos had already returned. The prisoners were already in roll-call formation in front of the blocks. From all sides people were yelling at them to hurry and raising their fists in menace, so they dragged the wagon half running, with every SS man they passed still managing to land a few telling blows.

Panting, they reached the quarantine block, left the wagon and ran upstairs. In the corridors the others had long since lined up for roll call. Curses were coming at them from all directions and all the room orderlies were hitting them. As if it was their fault they'd been forced to work so long!

The roll call was very slow. The SS man had long since come and gone and they were still standing there waiting. Hans felt dizzy. His heart wouldn't stop racing. His throat stayed choked shut and his grazed feet were burning so badly he had tears in his eyes. And if he squatted for a moment or tried to lean on the bunks behind him, there was always a 'comrade' to immediately give him a poke so that he jumped back to attention.

After roll call, fetching bread, which again meant seemingly endless lining up. Then the bread and the coffee. A little bit of jam smeared on the bread. He licked it off. He drank the coffee, but couldn't get the bread down his throat. Later . . . After he'd been able to lie down for a while . . . His appetite would come back then. He undressed in preparation and lay down on the bed. Sleep came over him as salvation, liberation from the strap that had bound him to the wagon. The shovel had been taken out of his hands at last. All pain was stilled and longing hushed because he had sunk deep into the dark pool of unconsciousness.

Suddenly a yell, a shock: '*Alles aufstehen!*'

What was happening? Pure confusion as thoughts formed again from the fathomless depths. Was that Mother calling? Was there a fire? Was he ill? Running a fever? He could hardly move. Then his mind cleared. The Russian he shared his bed with was giving him a good shaking. 'Foot inspection!'

What? Now? Exhausted and miserable, he had been overwhelmed by sleep and hadn't washed. Now it was the middle of the night and his feet were dirty. But this time he was in luck. The SS man was drunk and couldn't see straight. He walked past Hans, who was allowed to lie down again half an hour later and went back to sleep immediately.

He wasn't rested at four o'clock that morning. All of his muscles, the skin over his whole body – pain everywhere. He hoped he wouldn't be put to work again. But it was a vain hope. No sooner were they lined up than the room orderly came in with a note. He had the detail's numbers and Hans had to go out again.

Now it would be a whole day. Eleven hours of loading gravel, carting gravel, unloading gravel. Sometimes with a little variation: spreading the gravel over a new section of street or sieving the old road surfacing. Then pulling the wagon again.

Hans held up under it. He kept working even though his back seemed about to burst open, even though the shovel in his hands seemed to be made of glowing lead. It was the only correct attitude, because when the Poles saw that he wasn't giving up, they gradually became a little more accommodating and now and then one of them even took his shovel from him. But that was hardly an advantage, those few minutes of rest, because when he had to start again he was so stiff that every movement used up two or three times as much energy.

Still, he got through that day too, and the next day and the fourth, and the days passed without too many incidents. A blow, a snarl, cursing. But who counts any of that? Or the exhaustion and pain, only increasing, what did they matter? The grazes on his feet started to fester. The *Sanitäter* put some Sepso on it – an iodine surrogate – but what would that help? His eyes were inflamed from the sun and the sand, but so what?

The one time he did report to sick parade in the morning the Sanitäter laughed at him. 'For a few miserable little scrapes like that?'

And then the hunger! Constant hunger! What, after all, is a single ration of bread and a litre of soup a day? And what kind of soup! Water with some beets in it, or chopped turnips. Now and then, one and a half potatoes per litre of soup and they were always at the bottom of the kettle, which the room orderlies reserved for themselves and their friends. Sometimes you could get your hands on another litre through a friend or good fortune, but it was better not to eat it. It was definitely better not to eat too much soup because now, after one or two weeks, all of the old prisoners – in a camp, that means between forty and forty-five – had oedema of the legs. What would become of him if he got oedema, with these wounds? They would never heal!

On the fifth day, as they were dragging the fully loaded wagon: the incident! There on the left, women coming down a side street. They were ordered to stop the wagon fifty metres from the intersection to make sure none of the men came into contact with the women.

Hans held his breath, peering intently. Then, losing all self-control, a cry: 'Friedel!' He threw off his strap and ran towards the women. But he had only gone a step or two when someone grabbed him. It was Leib, the Polish Jew, who brought him back to his senses.

'*Du Idiot*, they'll beat you till you can't even stand up any more!'

55

Hans said he didn't care.

'They'll beat her too.'

That convinced him. Nervously he looked at the Block-ältester, who was supervising the work but hadn't noticed anything. He had walked ahead a little to watch the girls.

Still, Friedel had seen him and waved from the distance, cautiously, with a slight movement of one hand. It seemed to him that she was trying to say, *I'm still here. Do you think of me sometimes?* And he answered, *Oh, I am so tired, too tired to think of you.*

But you have *to think of me, because that's the only way you'll be able to stick it out.*

That was true and he waved back cautiously, as if to signal that he'd understood, that she was right, and that he would keep on fighting with her image before him.

Even harder days came. The weather changed, turning colder. At first it was a relief. His skin didn't smart as much, his muscles felt a little more supple and he didn't get out of breath as quickly as in the heat. But then the rain came. His clothes offered no protection: a linen coat and a vest. He was soaked to the skin.

But that wasn't the worst. After two days of rain there was nothing left of the road. The entire route to the pile of gravel was a succession of ponds and mounds of muddy clay. The water was over their ankles. Their shoes got sucked down into the mud and the wheels sank in gunge up to the axles.

But they had to keep the wagon moving. And if it got stuck in the mud with its load of gravel, the Blockältester's stick knew what to do. And if the Blockältester wasn't able to rage hard enough to get the wagon loose, an SS man who was better at it would come along. He'd wade through the muck in his boots and give the closest man a kick that sent mud flying around everyone's ears. Then they'd grab the spokes of the wheels and tug and twist, and the Sturmmann would bellow and lash out, and the Blockältester would laugh to show how much he admired the Sturmmann's energetic approach. And so they got the wagon moving again after all. Because although the men were wet and tired, one or two weeks hadn't been enough to fully deplete their energy reserves, and when they had to, they could. They all had scrapes and lumps from the blows they'd received, but so far none of them had been really hurt.

But they knew that wasn't something you could rely on. Just yesterday they had seen the Blockführer, the SS man in charge of the blocks, hit a Gypsy boy so hard his whole cheek burst open. He hadn't been standing straight enough. After the roll call they'd had to take him to the Krankenbau.

You heard about people being beaten and wounded almost every day. That was why Hans and the other men put in even more effort. Faced with the furious SS man, and with everyone in equal danger, a sense of solidarity arose after all. The Poles encouraged Hans, and Hans did his best to help the Poles. They no longer felt the pain from the blows, only grim determination. They would get the wagon out! 'Hau ruck! Hau ruck!'

Fifteen pairs of arms succeeded where two horses would have certainly failed. But at this stage they were still strong, they still had energy reserves. What would it be like in a week, in a month? Hans worried in bed at night. He felt ill. He had taken off the wet vest but a fever made him shiver under the one small blanket he had to share with two others. Despite the warmth, despite the many people crammed in together, he was shivering. What would he be like tomorrow?

The Poles, who had already been there for several weeks, often received packages from home. The Russians often got food from friends in the camp; nobody was as skilled at 'organizing' as a Russian. Even if ten SS men were standing near the kitchen, a Russian wasn't scared and always managed to filch a bag of potatoes. And he always managed to make a concealed fire to cook them. But nowhere was there as much comradeship as among the Russians either, because that same Russian always had a friend in quarantine to share his booty with.

But who looked after Hans? Or the handful of other Dutchmen in quarantine? He had already noticed that the Dutch weren't held in high regard in the camp. Whether Jews or non-Jews, the Dutch were seen as weak and lazy.

Maybe they were right. The Dutch are calm and business-like. They're not used to being overzealous, using underhand practices to pursue their goals or letting themselves be rushed along. And why should they be zealous about this drudgery? It was either pointless, in which case zeal was insane, or it was a war industry, and then laziness was an obligation.

But as a result almost none of the Dutch prisoners had a position where they could organize anything. Not one worked in the kitchen block or the storerooms and, with the possible exception of Leen Sanders, the few who had anything showed precious little community spirit.

Friedel did manage to smuggle in a few more packages of bread for him. Again they felt like a blessing beyond any he'd ever received before. But how could that help with this hunger, with this work? How much longer could he last?

After three weeks: the surprise. It was still very early, and Hans was nibbling the small slice of bread he had saved from yesterday for the third time, when the block clerk came into the room. He called out numbers. Including Hans's.

Four of them stood together in the corridor and, after the Kommandos had left, they went to the Krankenbau. There was already a whole group of prospective Pfleger in Block 21.

Hans got into a conversation with a little old man. At first sight he looked fat, but on closer inspection you saw how swollen he was. The 'fat' was all water; on his forehead he had a large boil. His name was Cohn. He was a dermatologist and had been working in a roadworks Kommando for a month already. This was the third time he had had to come to see the Lagerarzt and he was sure that he would be turned away again this time too.

Hans was feeling more optimistic and his instincts were correct. A few short questions about his training and so on, and then he felt that it was going to be all right. Back to the Krankenbau after all, another chance after all. The wagon, the gravel, being overworked, spending entire days in the rain – all that was over. And despite his rough hands – he couldn't even write a note any more – despite the wounds on his feet, despite his back, which he could neither bend nor stretch, he returned to Block 28 and the admissions ward full of courage and fighting spirit.

CAN YOU IMAGINE THAT you can also get bored in a concentration camp? Hans was bored. There was no work for them in Block 28. They had to wait until they were assigned to the different hospital blocks where Pfleger were required.

Hans wouldn't have minded getting some rest – lying on his bed until late in the morning; going out into the autumn sun in the afternoon – but that wasn't possible either. After all, the principle of a concentration camp was *Bewegung*: even if there wasn't anything to do, you had to keep moving at all times.

Getting up in the morning to the sound of the gong, washing and dressing, and then, when the work gong rang three-quarters of an hour later, starting work. The room orderlies mopped the floor. You weren't allowed to help because then the room orderlies wouldn't have any work left and would get put into who-knows-what kind of heavy outside Kommando.

Then, cleaning windows again. Armed with a piece of newspaper or some other kind of scrap paper, you began at six in the morning. At noon, when the soup arrived, you had cleaned two windows. If you did it too quickly you had to make them dirty again and start over – woe betide you if the Blockältester or an SS man came near and you weren't industriously cleaning. A snarl and a blow was the least you could expect, but they could also tell you that they had no use for a lazy Pfleger and that you had to go and stand 'next to the bell' the next morning. That meant falling in outside the blocks the next morning at the second gong. You had to go and stand under the gong to be assigned to a different Kommando.

That was why they cleaned their windows industriously.

Hans was still very content. The work was boring and spending the whole day on your feet was tiring, but it didn't sap your strength. The soup in the Krankenbau was often a little better than in quarantine and it was mostly possible to get half a litre extra because a lot of the Polish Pfleger, who received enormous packages, didn't eat the *Lagersuppe* at all.

In general, roll call in the camp dragged on for ever. Sometimes the men had to stand in the rain for two or more hours. The Krankenbau did its own count, however, which was always completed in a few minutes. Then, after roll call, you could go to sleep or walk or do something else as you wished. There were no foot inspections or similar harassments. Pfleger are presumed to be able to keep themselves clean enough.

It was possible to live. And, most importantly for him, he was in touch with Friedel again. The evenings were growing shorter and in the twilight he could generally find someone who was willing to go with him as a lookout so that he could talk to her at the window for a few minutes.

'Friedel, I don't need any more food from you. I'm getting extra soup every day now.'

'What good is that soup going to do you?'

'Today I earned a ration of bread. I washed some underwear for a fat Pole.'

Friedel ran a nervous hand over her centimetre-long hair. They were silent. Yelling came from the room behind Friedel.

A little later: 'The block clerk was on to us. But she didn't see that it was me who was talking.'

'How are things there?'

'Oh, Hans, we don't have to work. We get extra rations just like the people doing hard labour. That makes it doable, but ...'

'But what?' he insisted.

'Oh, it's all so sinister here. Now with those Greek girls again. What exactly it is, I don't know. They've been burnt internally. There were fifteen of them. After the treatment they were in terrible pain. One has died.'

'Are you sure they're not going to do something like that to you too?'

'Those experiments seem to be over. Last week there was someone called Professor Schumann, a fat Jerry, but I don't see him any more now. I think they've started on something else, something with injections down below.'

'Won't they take you for that, then?'

'Maybe not. I'm a nurse now on the ward with all the Dutchwomen and they don't tend to take the staff as quickly.'

Then they had to stop again because that familiar high-pitched whistle was sounding through the camp.

Every evening the Rapportführer entered the camp. He was a dangerous fellow, *Oberscharführer* Claussen. He always carried a riding crop. If you got close to him and only received a lash with the whip, you were getting off lightly. When he entered the camp a shrill, high-pitched whistle from the Häftlinge sounded as a warning. Everyone who heard it passed it on, and no matter how much it annoyed Claussen, he never managed to catch any of the whistlers in the act.

But he still vented his rage, taking it out on anyone he could pick fault with: if your hair was too long, if you hadn't stood to attention rigidly enough, if you smiled, or if he simply didn't like the look of you. Not an evening passed without at least one man getting a severe beating, and even that was a moderate state of affairs compared to places like Buna or Birkenau, the so-called Auschwitz II.

This place, Auschwitz I, was the model camp. The blocks were brick and there were beds for everyone. This was where the big storehouses were, where a little extra for everyone could be filched now and then, and where the model hospital was. No, the conditions in Auschwitz I were not indicative of the Auschwitz complex in general. Not according to the fellow Hans spoke to that evening. He had arrived with Hans last month and had been sent to Buna in the group of 228 men. It was two hours by foot: an enormous industrial complex with building sites everywhere.

Most of the lads had to lay cables; some of them were in the concrete Kommando. It wasn't easy, lugging 75-kilo bags of cement all day, and at the double. Hans should try to imagine how you felt in the evenings. They had to carry the bags a distance of more than a hundred metres, from the narrow-gauge railway to the concrete mixers, and every ten metres there was a Kapo or an SS man swinging his fists to keep the pace up. There was a fatality right away on the very first day.

Did Hans remember Plaut, the registered nurse from Westerbork, a very capable fellow? They played the old trick on him. There were guards posted at the four corners of the grounds they were working on; you weren't allowed to cross those lines. The SS man ordered Plaut to fetch a small box that was outside of those bounds. When Plaut hesitated, he hit him on the head with a shovel. He had no choice but to go and get the box, but as soon as he crossed the line between the guard posts, they shot him.

'Don't say a word to his wife. She's here in Block 10. The next day it was old Jacobson, a forty-five-year-old – in camp terms, that's ancient. He was jogging along in the hot, suffocating afternoon and collapsed under his seventy-five kilos. Anyone who tried to help him was driven away with blows with a stick. After half an hour they let someone look at him. He was dead.

'We wanted to carry away the body, but that wasn't allowed because he'd been counted when we'd turned out in the morning and the number had to be right in the evening as well. So we dragged the body with us to the evening roll call so it could be counted again. Now, after five weeks, twenty of our lads are already dead and that will go faster and faster because everyone is exhausted and we all have wounds.

'Just yesterday, Joop van Dijk. Built like this, but lugging the bag of cement, he had to stop for a moment to catch his breath. The guard saw him, hit him with his rifle butt, then kicked him in the head when he was on the ground. Joop just lay there, unconscious. He must have landed badly because when we went to take him back with us in the evening he still hadn't regained consciousness. There was blood coming out of his ear. Nobody could help him. First we had to line up for roll call. During roll call he came round a little, groaning and asking for water. He kept it up for about two hours. Then, finally, at the end of the roll call, they took him to hospital. This morning he was dead.'

'How did you get here?' Hans asked.

'Yesterday evening I reported to the hospital. I had a temperature and a sore throat. They said I had diphtheria and people with contagious diseases aren't allowed to stay there. That's why I've been brought here to the central hospital. I'm glad of it too. That infirmary in Buna is a terrible place. The beds are triple bunks, like here, but they put the worst cases on top, supposedly to give them more air. Last night there was a dysentery patient with severe diarrhoea above me. He spent the whole night yelling for a bedpan. There was nobody to help him, of course, so he kept doing it in bed. Towards morning it started to leak through. I crawled over to one side as far as I could to avoid getting it all over me. When the Pfleger came and saw what had happened, he started hitting the fellow. Right in the face, at least five times. The Pfleger is fat. He dishes out the soup and serves himself from the bottom of the kettle. If someone dies – and that's a couple of people every day – there's bread left over. If someone gets moved to a different ward or hospital, they don't send the bread on. That Pfleger in Buna is eating my ration of bread for tonight right now. Anyway, my throat's too sore to swallow it.'

'So you're lucky to have diphtheria?'

'I'm not so sure. I reckon everyone who ends up in Auschwitz hospital goes from here to the gas chamber.'

No, Hans didn't believe that. The Lagerarzt did come from time to time, but they didn't take strong young men away with them.

'Can you get a message to my wife?' the man asked.

'Did you have children?'

'No.'

'Then she'll be in Block 10, like all the women from our transport. It's too dangerous in the daytime, but I can try tomorrow evening. What's your name again?'

'Have you forgotten? Boekbinder, the Zionist leader.'

Hans remembered now, and they talked about Zionism and subjects like that for a while; even if you're up to your neck in filth, you don't want to completely degenerate.

Hans was no Zionist: 'There is no special Jewish issue, just general social issues, general social contradictions that are taken out on Jews. If those problems were thrashed out once and for all, the Jewish question would automatically cease to exist.'

'But the Jews who cling to their own religion and traditions will always remain a foreign element.'

'Even if that's the case, what does it matter? In Russia dozens of ethnic groups with their own cultures, small and large, live alongside each other without conflict.'

But their hearts weren't in the conversation and Hans was glad when the gong rang: nine o'clock, time to go to sleep.

In admissions, the diphtheria patients' bunks were next to those of the *Reservepfleger*. That was no cause of concern. After all, they were all going to end the same way. Unless the Allies suddenly appeared. Who would still be alive? Ah, it was all taking so long, too long for them, and there was that ball of clay again, the one that lodged in his thoughts and, like a golem, sometimes became a separate entity, holding long discourses on life and death. But Hans now knew the magic word that broke the golem's spell: 'Friedel'. Because she existed, the golem was silenced. Hans summoned up her image and the ball of clay shrank and became lifeless again.

He grew calmer. Where there had been fear and doubt, he now felt a quiet longing, and with that he fell asleep.

H E HAD BEEN IN Block 28 for a fortnight when instructions came one afternoon: 'All Reservepfleger fall in.'

What was it this time? The Blockältester came into admissions with a well-dressed Häftling, a real prominent. The man was wearing a black jacket and a black beret. His striped trousers were of a woolly material. The full prominent style. They talked a little between themselves and the stranger said that he could use five of them.

'Take six,' the Blockältester said, 'otherwise I'll never get rid of them.'

They picked out six of the lads including four Dutchmen: Hans, the young psychologist Gerard van Wijk, Tony Haaksteen, who had a bachelor's in medicine, and Van Lier, the junior doctor. They had to gather up their things and go with the man, who turned out to be the new Blockältester of Block 9. He was friendly and told them that he had already spent nine years in concentration camps. As a Communist he had been picked up in the first year of Hitler's regime. He was now fifty.

'Oh, camp life's bearable once you've got a bit used to it. You know, ninety per cent die in the first year, but if you get through that, you can manage the rest too. You get used to the food, you get clothes that are a little better and once you're an *Alter Häftling*, the SS has a bit of respect for you.'

'But don't you want to get out again?' Hans asked.

'Wanting it's one thing. It's not so much fun on the outside either. I'm a carpenter. Am I supposed to start all over again with a boss at my age? In the camp I'm my own boss.'

'I thought the SS was the boss.'

'Oh, they're all little brats. I was already in Oranienburg* when they were still in nappies. The camp isn't a camp any more. It's a sanatorium. You're Dutch, aren't you? I've had dealings with Dutchmen before. That was, let me see, in 1941 in Buchenwald. Four hundred Dutch Jews. I was Blockältester in the quarantine block. They were with me for three months and had already got a bit used to it. I made sure they didn't have to work too hard. After all, they were better lads than the Poles and their sort. Then the whole troop was suddenly sent to Mauthausen. I heard later that they ended up in a gravel pit. Carting gravel up the slope at double time the whole day long. The toughest ones stuck it out for five weeks.'

He was right. Hans remembered the story from Amsterdam. In February Hendrik Koot, a member of the *WA*, was beaten to death in the Jewish quarter. In retaliation the Grüne Polizei rounded up four hundred young men off the streets. A couple of months later the first death notices came. The others didn't last much longer.

Meanwhile they had arrived at Block 9. They had to wait in the corridor for a while and were then shown into Room 1.

Sitting on the other side of the table was a short, thickset man wearing a red triangle with a P on it. A Polish political prisoner, in other words. He had a round fat head and a hard

* A concentration camp in Brandenburg, Germany. One of the first the Nazis established when they gained power in 1933.

mouth, but a gentle, somewhat distracted look in his eyes. Nervously he fidgeted with a pencil. He was sure to have been through a lot and might have been in the camp a long time too.

The lads had to report to him one by one. As the acting Blockältester and senior doctor in the block, he would be allocating the jobs.

First up was Tony Haaksteen. Was he a doctor? He tried to evade the question a little. Then the block doctor asked him how old he was. Twenty-two. The bystanders laughed and there were mumbled comments along the lines of *blöde Holländer*. Then it was the turn of Gerard van Wijk, who said that he had studied medicine and was now a psychologist. The block doctor didn't entirely understand. So he was a psychiatrist? Gerard didn't dare say no.

'Go to Room 3 then. To your compatriot Polak – they couldn't use him in Buna. That's where the madmen are.'

Hans felt like the ground had been cut from under his feet. After all, he had been a psychiatric intern for two years and was a lot closer to being a psychiatrist than Gerard, the theoretician. But trying to compete didn't seem sensible. Maybe Gerard's only chance was as a 'psychiatrist'. Accordingly, Hans called himself an internist.

'Fine,' the boss said. 'Just stay here, in this room. This is the admissions doctor, Ochodsky. You can assist him a bit.' Van Lier didn't get a hearing. The Blockältester from 28 had already told his new colleague at 9 that Van Lier had a foot wound. As a result he had to go to a hospital ward first until the wound had healed.

Hans was delighted. Assisting the admissions doctor – that had to be a good job.

He still hadn't grasped anything about how things worked. Who practised medicine in the Lager? The lads of eighteen and twenty who ruled the roost in outpatients and sold the medicine for cigarettes and margarine. Not to those who needed it, but to those who could afford it.

Who was in charge of Block 9? Not the Blockältester and the Blockarzt, but the quartermaster and his cronies: Polish ruffians in cohorts with the odd Russian.

Medical work? Dr Ochodsky, who was good to the bone, had nothing to do himself. There were about ten admissions a day and Ochodsky told them which ward to go to. That was five minutes' work; otherwise he spent the whole day on his bed. When the doorkeeper raised the alarm, he knew an SS man was approaching and quickly began examining someone. No, there wasn't any medical work, but there was enough work. Still, Block 9 had another, inestimable advantage. After all, as sure as night follows day, 9 is always followed by 10!

IT WAS FOUR THIRTY. 'Get up! Gong!' the night watchman shouted as he turned on the light in the staff room. Almost all of them shot up. Yesterday Paul, the Blockältester, had ranted and raved so much at a couple of men who were still in bed five minutes after the gong that nobody was brave enough to turn over again today. Only Gerard stayed lying there for a moment.

'Get up!' Hans urged him. 'Do you want to have to drag kettles around for an extra week?'

'Oh, Hans, I can't. I slept so badly. There's no straw left in my mattress and I've been coughing so much.'

'It's a bad cough, but not having any straw is your own fault. Yesterday there were five bales at Block 21.'

Gerard really didn't have much get-up-and-go when it came to things like that. He didn't stick up for himself. But what could you expect from a lad like that? A respectable middle-class family, son of a civil servant. They hadn't been wealthy, but they'd never had to struggle to get by either. How could someone like that stand up to all these Häftlinge? They were a nice bunch, the people you spent your days with: black marketeers, pickpockets and other antisocial elements. Any political Poles among them had been in the camp for years and were no longer exactly kind-hearted.

They experienced that again after they'd hurriedly got up and were standing in the corridor half dressed.

'What kept you, you bloody scum, you pathetic Hollanders?' Kuczemba, the quartermaster, had a shove ready for both of them; that was your 'good morning'. Then you had to trot off to the kitchen and pick out a big kettle of tea. If you came back with a small kettle, they'd curse you up and down or make you go back again, and if you came with a large kettle, half would end up getting thrown out – there was always more boiled ditchwater available than the patients wanted. They raced in four pairs to the kitchen block, where twenty men from other blocks were already waiting.

In the kitchen, more racket. The Unterscharführer had just caught a Russian organizing some potatoes. Not satisfied with beating the Russian bloody, he had immediately dealt with a couple of cooks and the doorkeeper too. That was why they weren't allowed to wait inside, but had to stay outside until the tea had been poured into the kettles.

It was cold, snow was whirling through the courtyard and their feet were already wet. Soon they would be soaked to the skin. A vest and a linen coat didn't offer much protection. They pressed back against the plastered wall, sheltering from the worst of the snow under the eaves. But the Unterscharführer was coming their way again.

'What are you doing there, you filthy swine? Attention!' Gerard, who didn't line up fast enough, got a nice little kick on the ankle. A little kick, but how was he supposed to carry his kettle now? As if that bothered anyone. And so Van Dam MD and the young psychologist Van Wijk stood there freezing on that wet, overcast November morning.

'Why do we have to wait so long?' Gerard asked.

'You'd be better off asking why we had to leave the block so fast. You know what it's like by now: "*Bewegung, Bewegung, los, Eile!"* They hurry you up on principle, to make you waste as much energy as possible.'

After half an hour the chilled men were finally let into the kitchen. The kettles were steaming hot. The warm, damp air penetrated their clothes, reviving them a little. The cooks were standing next to the kettles in grimy white uniforms. Big Poles, brash and brawny. You had to make sure not to go too close; they'd been working for hours under constant harassment and provocation.

Now the Kapo was at it again: *'Du Drecksau,* you're spilling half of it! You want me to smash your face in for you?'

The Pole shrugged. The Kapo was a German with a green triangle, the symbol for imprisoned criminals. He could have five murders on his conscience, but the SS had made him the supervisor and you just had to put up with it.

Hans and Gerard had picked out a kettle and put the iron braces for carrying it underneath. Hans spotted a barrel of salt and remembered that Friedel had asked him if he could get her some. But as he was sticking a handful in his pocket, a stream of cold water hit him in the face. A cook who was rinsing out a kettle had caught him at it. Now he was sopping wet after all. But that, too, was something he would survive. He looked at the cook and grinned vacantly. How were you supposed to respond to being sprayed like that? Hit back? Madness. The cook was much stronger than him, well fed and, what's more, in the right. If you catch someone organizing, you're allowed to punish them on the spot.

They picked up the kettle and trudged out of the kitchen. After just twenty-five metres Gerard had to put it down again. He wasn't strong, a slight youth who'd never done any physical work, and the kettle weighed more than a hundred kilos.

Finally they staggered into the block. By then it must have been about six o'clock – only the Blockältester had a watch, but you got a sense of time. In another hour, Block 10 would open and he still had a lot to do.

Janus, the Stubenältester, had already started mopping the floor when Hans came in. It was a small ward with twenty-eight patients, all Poles and Russians – 'Aryans'. They slept in triple bunks. The ones in the top bunks got the most warmth; the bottom bunks had the most fleas, because although fleas are good at jumping, gravity makes them fall back down again. This was why the top bunks were occupied by the prominents: leading figures in Poland, many with titles and decorations, political prisoners who were held in high esteem by their fellow inmates. The lower bunks were occupied by simple folk, farmers and workers who had illegally slaughtered a pig, shouted out a swear-word at a German soldier, or often not done anything at all they were aware of.

Living among these people wasn't easy for Hans. The prominents were demanding, often refusing to submit to camp discipline, not wanting to get up at half past four to go and wash, wanting to keep food in their bed, and deeply in-sulted if you said anything about it when they threw onion peel and other rubbish down on the floor.

The ordinary people in the middle and lower bunks made no effort at all to conceal their anti-Semitism. Hans was glad he couldn't understand what they said about him but you felt something like that. He didn't let it get to him too much. What difference did it make?

He looked out of the window just in time to see the prisoners lugging the tea kettles for Block 10 up from

Block 19. Fortunately Janus wasn't a bad chap and let Hans go. He ran outside. As long as the Blockältester didn't come now. No, the coast was clear. A Greek from Block 19 was happy to let Hans take over from him. Hans was happy too. Panting nervously, he hauled the kettle up the steps and into Block 10.

There wasn't a single woman in the corridor. Yes, just one, a girl really. She looked sideways at the men, but ran away when the doorkeeper appeared. They carried their kettle over to the staircase that led up to the first floor. The stairs were crowded with women jostling to collect tea. A fat Slovakian Stubenälteste was blocking the stairs.

'Nobody comes downstairs! Back, back, you *blöde Sauen*!' She shoved the women and beat them back and Hans started feeling faint at heart. How would he ever reach Friedel? But there was Betty; she saw him and raced upstairs. It took so long, and the doorkeeper was already shouting, 'Men, out! Go on, go!' He wouldn't get to see Friedel, not this time. Yes, he would! She was coming.

She worked her way through the throng on the stairs and came up against the Slovakian. Then Hans leapt over to her: 'My wife, let her, one minute.' The Slovakian took her hand off the rail and Friedel jumped down the last steps.

He grabbed her hand. She went to kiss him, but he was too frightened. For a moment they couldn't speak. She pulled herself together first.

'Hans, any news?'

'No, Friedel, nothing.'

'Do you get enough to eat?'

'Yes, you can have some of my bread if you need it. A Pole gave me some from a package.'

'No, sweetheart, you eat it. You work hard. I don't do a thing all day. Waiting and waiting. Still, my luck's been holding out. Others . . .' Her voice caught.

'What?' he insisted.

She looked around nervously. 'They injected Loulou and Ans yesterday.'

For a second he bit his lip. He understood why she was so nervous. They didn't know what exactly the injections were, but they were definitely awful. Friedel told him that Ans especially had had dreadful abdominal pain. She'd bled all night. The blood had come with cramps, ten times as much as a normal period. And now she was lying on her bed, wretched and exhausted, and next week she'd have to go back to see the professor again.

They were both silent. But in their eyes was the fear that one day she too would have to undergo the same thing.

Then the doorkeeper came. During her confinement in the camp she had forgotten how to talk and could only shout. That was what made her such a good doorkeeper. 'Get out! Are you mad? All the men have left. If the *Aufseherin* comes, it'll be my head!' She screamed so loudly the Aufseherin was bound to come and that was why it was better to go.

Now Friedel could no longer control herself. She pressed herself against him and kissed him and kissed him and he kissed her back. The doorkeeper was beside herself and threatened to get the Blockälteste. That was why Hans pushed Friedel away and forced himself to calm down.

'Friedel, be brave.'

'I am brave, but it's so miserable for those girls.'

'I understand, but that won't last for ever either.'

'How much longer?'

'I don't know, darling. It will all turn out all right.'

What else could he say? What else could he predict? Friedel was pure gold, but gold is a soft metal, and if she had been made of steel it might not have been so easy for all this suffering to leave its traces on her.

He walked away, fleeing really, because he felt so powerless to comfort her. What help were words in the face of such deeds? Hans had a good inkling of what was going on in Block 10 and why. Wasn't mass sterilization one of the Germans' goals? Wouldn't they like to be able to sterilize all Jews, Poles, Russians and possibly others? What could these gynaecological experiments be if not attempts at sterilization? Jewish women were cheap guinea pigs. One could only delight in their suffering and if they died a miserable death it hardly mattered at all. In this dark mood, he returned to Block 9.

HE DIDN'T RECEIVE A warm welcome. Paul was waiting for him in the corridor and began swearing furiously the moment he saw Hans coming in.

He went through his entire repertoire: '*Himmel, Arsch und Zwirn, Herr Gott Sakrament, du verfluchter Idiot*, just walking off in work time. You've been in that whorehouse next door, haven't you? I don't understand how they can set up something like that in a respectable KZ. In Buchenwald I literally didn't see a skirt for five years until they opened the brothel.'*

Zielina, the head doctor, who was standing next to him, gave him a thump: 'But then you were there every day, I suppose.'

'What do you think? I didn't go there once. I might be a Communist, one of those cursed red pigs, but you won't find me around whores. Anyway, they never got the better class of customer there in Buchenwald. Don't imagine for a minute you'd have seen a red triangle – a political prisoner – going into the brothel there. I don't understand what kind of spineless characters we have here in Auschwitz. They're queuing up there all evening.'

'The food's too good here,' Zielina mocked.

* The Nazis established brothels in concentration camps to encourage prisoners to cooperate, though no Jewish male prisoners were allowed to use them. Female prisoners were forced into prostitution. In Auschwitz the brothel was located in Block 24.

'But getting back to this emaciated streak of misery,' Paul continued, returning to Hans. 'I'll laugh my head off if the Rapportführer bumps into you there one day. You know what they did to Florek, our barber, don't you?'

'No.'

'Florek was standing by the window conversing with one of those ladies from Block 10. You know what Florek's like – the requisite filthy chat, the requisite filthy gestures. And who should come along but Kaduk, the second Rapportführer. He grabs him by the back of the neck, makes a meatball of his face and then marches him off to the Blockführerstube, where he reported him to Hössler, the Lagerführer: twenty-five on the backside. He got that helping right away – in the bunker with the pizzle.'

'What's that?'

'Just what I said: a dried bull's pizzle – a first-class Germanic disciplinary device. Florek had to lie on his stomach for three whole days. He still doesn't dare to sit down properly and it's been two weeks already.'

'Haven't you ever heard of "The Land of Twenty-Five"?' Zielina interrupted. 'That was German South-East Africa. The standard punishment for the Negroes there was twenty-five of the best with a whip or a cane. So the whole country got it as a nickname.'

Paul said, 'We Germans just happen to be a savage nation.' He glared at Hans with a terribly fierce expression, swore a little more and then sent him off to Block 21. Because that was what the fuss was all about: there was a transport Kommando that day.

There were already fifteen men standing by Block 21. The doorkeeper gestured frantically, pushing the men into rows of five and madly cursing the blocks who still hadn't sent their contingent of labourers.

It was all '*Schnell! Los! Tempo!*' but after the thirty men had been drummed up, it still took another half-hour for the SS guard to arrive. And when they'd finally marched out of the gate and arrived at the *SS-Krankenrevier*, there were no wagons for them to use. The *Rottenführer* started negotiating and they stood there waiting for another hour. It was cold, bitterly cold, and they were shivering in their linen suits in the middle of the street; the pavements, where prisoners swept away the snow, were reserved for the SS going in and out of the buildings. Three large buildings: *SS-Revier, SS-Standortverwaltung Süd-Ost* and the *Kommandantur*.

These were real beehives, with men swarming in and out, along with the occasional young woman in smart clothes that had undoubtedly belonged to some – now murdered – young Jewish lady. Sometimes there were also Häftlinge from the Kommando SS-Revier, who worked in the SS hospital as cleaners, with some prominents even working as chemists or dental technicians. They were well off. They ate SS food and had all the toiletries and medicine they needed. The Kommando SS-Revier was the camp's most important source of medicine. The Häftlinge who worked there smuggled it into the camp, where they sold it in exchange for margarine, sausage and clothes that others, in turn, had stolen from the Bekleidungskammer. All of the medicaments taken from the thousands who arrived on the trains ended up here in the large attics and the enormous hospital dispensary. Together with the consignments from the *Sanitätslager der Waffen-SS* in Berlin-Lichtenberg, they formed an enormous stock. From this central point, the medicine was distributed to the entire SS across the south-eastern front. In the same way, the Auschwitz *Bauhof* was the distribution centre for building materials for all those troops, and the whole of the Waffen SS Süd-Ost was provided with war materials by Auschwitz factories. *DAW*, the *Deutsche Ausrüstungswerkstatte*, provided everything that was made of wood, munitions chests in particular. The munitions themselves were made at the 'Auto Union' and in the Buna factories. At Buna they also made synthetic rubber.

And here in these buildings was the headquarters of the enormous Auschwitz complex, which consisted of more than thirty camps: Auschwitz I – Hans's camp; Birkenau, the killing centre; Monowitz with the Buna factories; and many smaller camps with mining and agricultural Kommandos. Altogether more than 250,000 workers. All administered here in the Kommandantur and Standortverwaltung.

No, Auschwitz was more than torment writ large. With its factories and mines it was an important part of the Upper Silesian industrial area and its workers were cheaper than anywhere else in the world. They didn't need pay and they ate almost nothing. And then, when they were exhausted and fell victim to the gas chamber, there were still enough Jews and political opponents in Europe to make up the numbers yet again.

Berlin coordinated it all. In Wilhelmstrasse there was a special Concentration Camp Department under Himmler's command. There they arranged the transports to the camps through all of Europe. They were the ones who sent the order to Westerbork: so-many thousand to this or that camp. They calculated which percentage of the transport had to be exterminated immediately and how many people they needed as labourers.

Yes, Grün, the dentist, who had been in the camp for one and a half years, could explain exactly how it all worked. He was the model of a Pole who is not afraid of anything or anyone and never takes other people's interests into account. He was known all over the camp and always had the best jobs. His friends who worked in the political section had told him all kinds of secrets: command decisions, telegrams from Berlin. He had relationships with girls who worked at the SS-Revier, and when he got caught it didn't cost him his neck because he had another friend in the SS kitchen, who slipped him a litre of gin for the SS man who had found out too much about him. But now Grün's position was a little tenuous after all. It was like this: 'Do you know what *Faulgas* is?'

'No.'

'Faulgas is a Kommando of six hundred men – they live in Blocks 1 and 2. They walk five kilometres every day to a site where they're building a big plant next to a marsh to extract energy from the rotting sludge. There are civilian workers there too. Faulgas is the biggest Kommando for smuggling. The lads who work there take clothes and linen out with them, concealed under their uniforms, and sell them to the civilians for food. Watches and jewellery too. They get their merchandise from others who work in *Canada*. Everything from the trains goes there first; the people from Canada get a share of the takings.

'Two months ago I had a nice little deal going, but it went wrong. A fellow in Canada had found a couple of magnificent diamonds in the lining of a coat. He brought them to me because he knew I was in Faulgas. There was only one price for those diamonds: freedom.

'First I paid work-allocation a litre of schnapps and that got my mate into Faulgas too. Then we put out feelers with a Polish driver if he could mount a couple of boards under the bed of his lorry for the two of us to lie on. Between the crankshaft and the bed. But I had picked the wrong driver, because he was in with one of the guards. I happened to see the two of them talking and reported sick straight away. It cost me an arm and a leg, but the *Kommandoführer* ordered a guard to escort me back to camp. I wasn't even able to warn my friend. They beat him to death that same day. But they didn't find the diamonds on him because I'd already put them somewhere safe.

'You understand that since then I've been keeping a low profile because now there are definitely a few SS men out for those diamonds.'

Hans understood something else too. That when the deal went wrong, Grün sacrificed his friend and took off with the diamonds.

'If you want to shirk,' Grün continued, 'the Krankenbau's the best. Half a litre of spirits and you're a Pfleger.'

Grün definitely knew how to shirk.

The Rottenführer arrived. He had arranged a wagon. They had to pick up bags from the train and unload them here. Grün had a quick word with him and the Rottenführer gave him a pad and a pencil. He had to keep tally of the bags.

They set out with the wagon. It was fairly calm. They were all Pfleger with a black badge embroidered with the letters HKB on their left sleeve: *Häftlings-Krankenbau*. The Pfleger's letters were blue, technical staff had red and the doctors, white. But that division was theoretical, because here they were, all pushing the same wagon.

As a symbol, the HKB worked miracles. With all their aversion to intellectualism, the SS were still scared of it. Was it coincidence that the intellectuals at Westerbork were able to hold their own the longest and were then mostly sent to the privileged camp of Theresienstadt*? Was it coincidence that doctors, who are intimately involved in questions of life and death, had the best chance of survival not just in Auschwitz, but in other camps too?

Definitely not. Primitive man lives in constant fear of the spirit world, and that world is made up of the souls of the dead. If you beat someone to death, their soul will be hostile towards you, and the greater their spirit or mind was in life, the more dangerous they will be as a malevolent spirit after death. Especially dangerous are doctors, the stewards of the spiritual legacy passed on from ancient wizards who had power over the spirit realm of the living and the dead. And who could be more primitive than the *Übermensch*?

You had to be careful with doctors anyway. Even the greatest SS brute had an inner sense of 'you might need him one day.' That was what they owed it to, the doctors and the nursing and technical staff, their not being hurried too much and hardly hit at all.

But the work still had to be done and it was a nasty job. It was a goods wagon full of paper bags: 'Malarial mosquito poison' was printed on them followed by the chemical formula, a sulphur compound. A lot of the bags were torn and leaking fine green powder. When you picked them up, the powder went down your neck and formed a crust in the close-cropped

* A concentration camp/ghetto in occupied Czechoslovakia that was used partly for elderly and prominent Jews and was also presented to foreign visitors as a model camp.

hair on your sweaty head. It got in your nose, which started to run, and in your eyes, which began to water.

At first you did your very best to keep the bag in the middle of your back and not spill any, but each bag weighed fifty kilos, and once you were tired you had to put the bag on your shoulder and then it was liable to tilt. In no time they were covered with powder: clothes and faces green.

It was worst for your eyes, which stung and itched, and if you rubbed them with your dusty hands they started to burn. You were blinded and couldn't go on, and had to put the bag down for a moment. But you couldn't do that either, as the work had to be completed within the allocated time and that was the Rottenführer's responsibility, so he had to hurry you along. If you then complained about the wretched powder that hurt your eyes so much and stung your skin, the Rottenführer smiled enigmatically. He knew more than he was letting on.

When they got back to their blocks in the evening, exhausted and with bloodshot eyes, they all felt awful. One was shivery, the other nauseous, they all had sore eyes and some had come out in blisters. Hans felt ill; after roll call he went straight to bed. The next day he couldn't get up. He was running a temperature and the skin on his shoulders, back and everywhere the powder had reached was red and inflamed.

He was not the only one: four of the Pfleger had to stay in bed. Paul was quite reasonable. He sent others that day because the work had to go on.

The new workers asked the Rottenführer if they could get something made of rubber to put over their backs and shoulders, or goggles to protect their eyes. But the Rottenführer just shrugged. What did a few sick Häftlinge here or there matter?

One of the Pfleger had tried to bring a rubber sheet from a treatment room. The *SDG*, the SS orderly who inspected the hospital every day, bumped into him with it, gave him a few whacks and seized the sheet: 'Sabotage!'

Sabotage if you tried to conserve your health, if you tried to protect yourself from poison. The milk they give workers in paint factories in Holland must be a mortal sin. Anyway, that evening a few more of us were sick.

Paul looked concerned.

The next day was the same. Now seven of Block 9's thirty-five Pfleger were sick, just from the malaria powder. But the job was done.

Hans was not dissatisfied. The fever would pass, his body would excrete the poison and the patches of eczema that had formed everywhere would flake off. Meanwhile the rest was doing him good. The only bad thing was not being in touch with Friedel. He had sent her a note saying he wasn't well, but she hadn't been able to get an answer back to him. The lads who took the food to Block 10 were too scared. A few had just been beaten and one they'd found notes on had been sent to the *Strafkommando* in Birkenau.

THEN, ON THE FIFTH DAY: alarm! Paul came into the nurses' room: '*Los*, everyone get dressed, *Eile*! The Lagerarzt is in Block 19. He could be here any minute!'

They didn't know what was going on, but in the corridor Hans bumped into Grün. He looked very sombre. 'It's been going well for too long. He hasn't been for three weeks.'

In that moment the door opened. '*Achtung!*' shouted the doorkeeper.

Grün pulled Hans into the toilets with him. They heard the Lagerarzt going upstairs. Then a few of the sick Pfleger came into the toilets. Tony Haaksteen, the *Scheissmeister*, was about to start swearing at them, but Grün gestured for him to keep quiet.

'They've come here to hide, fathead.'

Grün couldn't suppress his curiosity. He took Hans upstairs with him. They slipped into the ward and went to stand among the other Pfleger. Almost all of the beds were empty and the men were lined up in the central corridor. The SDG wrote down the numbers of those who were severely ill and couldn't make it out of bed. When he was finished the inspection began.

It was disgusting, especially if you knew what it was about. The poor bags of bones, the worn-out, hollow-eyed skeletons, their bodies covered with wounds, standing stark-naked in a long line, leaning on each other or holding on to beds. The

Lagerarzt cast a quick glance at each of them and the SDG wrote down the numbers of everyone he pointed out – about half of them.

'What's that for?' one of the unfortunates dared to ask the Lagerarzt.

'*Halt's Maul.*'

But the SDG was a little more accommodating. 'The weak are going to a different camp. They have a special hospital there.'

The Pfleger within earshot sneered at each other. 'Special hospital, effective for all ailments.'

The Lagerarzt was finished and went downstairs. Hans felt a chill. Van Lier, the junior doctor, was in Room 3 with the madmen. He had been too cocky. Not only had he taken to bed with his inconsequential foot wounds, he'd also moved to a bunk among the madmen in Room 3 because two Dutchmen were working there, Van Wijk and Eli Polak, and he liked the company. If only they'd hidden him.

But after the Lagerarzt had left, Hans met Eli in the corridor. His face was stony. 'Only three – Reich Germans – are allowed to stay. They wrote down all the other numbers.'

'Van Lier's too?'

'Van Lier's too, with the insane.'

They went to see Paul, the Blockältester, to ask if there was anything he could possibly do. Paul was a strange fellow. He wasn't bad; he never hit anyone. He yelled and threatened, but never took it any further. But he'd been in the camp too long to know any pity. 'Van Lier? He was asking for it. He should have put in an effort. Why hasn't anything happened to either of you? You've worked here from the beginning and that's why I put you with the Pfleger – but that waste of space ...'

Of course, that wasn't an argument. After all, the Lagerarzt had accepted Van Lier as a Pfleger too. If Paul had something against him, he could have chased him out of bed or even – as Blockältester he had the right – discharged him from hospital. He shouldn't have let him walk into a trap like that. But after years in concentration camps even the best of people develop their own 'sense of justice'. They develop their own ticks. *Ein Vogel*, they call it.

Van Lier stayed on the list and left with the others the next day. At eleven o'clock the lorries arrived with a stream of SS men, the like of which Hans hadn't seen in the Krankenbau before. There was the Lagerführer with the two Rapportführer, the Lagerarzt with the SDG, the lorry drivers and many others. They gesticulated wildly and were especially rough and currish. No, this definitely didn't look like a transport to 'a special hospital,' as the SDG had put it.

The Blockältester was given a list with the names and numbers of the victims. They had to line up as quickly as possible, were given trousers and sandals, and were then rushed on to the lorries.

The most seriously ill, who couldn't walk, were carried down on stretchers by the Pfleger. If they didn't go fast enough, the Pfleger got a kick and the SS took charge of the unfortunate patient, who was thrown into the back of the lorry like a sack of flour.

These people weren't heavy. A man who was by nature a sturdy, solid fellow of say, 80 kilos, would now only weigh 50 or 52, and the wretches with a normal build weighed 38 at the most.

It's a law of nutrition that, even when wasting away, the heart, brain and organs maintain their normal weight the longest. As a result, most of them were all too aware of what was happening to them. They still had such a strong will to live. Many of them were crying and complaining to the Pfleger. A sixteen-year-old youth kicked up an enormous fuss. Then an SS man came and hit him with his belt. The boy screamed even louder; the SS man hit him harder still. German pedagogy was not, however, helpful.

Have you ever seen a drunk man kicking a howling dog? The dog starts howling even louder, and though the man is drunk he feels that the howling is justified and an indictment of his brutality. The man is not capable of a conscious sense of remorse, but the dog's complaints still arouse uncomfortable feelings in him, which he masks by increasingly brutal behaviour. Harder kicks, louder howls, until in the end the man kicks the dog to death. Finally it is no longer able to denounce him.

In the same way, the SS man hit harder and harder and the boy screamed louder and louder. In the end he picked him up and threw him into the back of the lorry like a ball. Then the boy was quiet. Hans stood in the downstairs corridor at the door to Room 1 and thought about it. No – you could never educate these 'people' to genuine remorse, even if they were one day called to account. 'A just punishment' would only engender greater hatred in them, and even if they pretended to be reformed, they would only conspire again as soon as they were set loose on humanity. For them, in the future, there could only be one possible punishment: death. That would be the only way to protect a new society.

Hans dug his nails into his flesh to restrain himself. Resistance, even a show of pity, would have been pointless suicide. During one of the previous 'selections', a Pfleger went to help one of the poor wretches. The SS supervisor did not approve of the whole process being delayed for a single bandage. The Pfleger objected. The Lagerarzt came up, wrote down the Pfleger's number and had him put on the lorry with the others.

Then Van Lier came down the corridor. Slowly he approached Hans. Wearing a filthy vest and clacking sandals, with his head bowed over his tall skinny body and swinging his long arms, he was the image of misery. It was as if death, who he was about to meet, had already taken up residence inside of him. He wanted to speak to Hans.

But Hans was at his wits' end and his courage failed him. He knew what Van Lier was going to ask, but he didn't know how to answer. That was why he turned away. It was a flight, a cowardly flight. He slunk off behind the big brick stove, but couldn't suppress his tormented curiosity and finally went back to the window.

They were ready now, the tailboards had been slammed shut, SS guards had climbed up on to the backs of the lorries, and the transport was about to drive off to Birkenau. Hans gripped the windowsill. He heard the Poles in their beds in loud discussion. He wanted to cry out, motivated by a vague feeling that someone would hear his cry and rush to help. But no sound made it past his lips. Silent tears welled up in his eyes. Then an arm wrapped around him. It was Zimmer, the fat Pole from Posen.

'Yes, son, they won't be complaining any more. Their song of woe is over.'

Hans shuddered; the man felt it.

'Come on, you have to be braver. You're in a very different position. You're fairly well off here in the room with us. You're young and strong, and you know the head doctor likes you.'

'You're right, Zimmer. But it's not for me, it's for those people going to slaughter so meekly.'

Zimmer smiled for a moment. 'Thousands have gone that way already. Millions. Did you cry then? It's only now it's right in front of your nose that you're so upset. But I don't blame you. You've seen so little. When the Germans invaded our country, in 1939, they marched straight into the Jews' houses. The men were driven into groups to be transported to labour camps, the women were raped. *Rassenschande*, a violation of their own race laws, but that didn't bother them.

'I saw them take little children by the feet and smash their heads against trees or doorposts. That was in fashion at the time. Every year there seems to be a new fashion in the SS. In 1940 it was the fashion to literally tear children apart. In '41 they'd take a tub of water and push the children's faces into it. They'd drown the poor little devils in ten centimetres of water. Lately they've calmed down a little. Now they kill the Jews with gas. The camps are sanatoriums compared to a couple of years ago, because they are killing people much more systematically now.'

'A lot must have happened in your region.'

'Don't talk to me about it, son. We Poles, we know the Germans. Over and over again they've hacked away at us, always dividing our country and annexing the best parts of it. Posen (Poznan in Polish), Danzig (that we know as Gdansk) and Stettin. They've gobbled up the most beautiful parts of Poland again now. But it doesn't matter where they set their borders. If they win the war, they'll enslave all of Poland. But they'll lose and when they do, justice will be ours.'

That was how he distracted Hans from the awful events that had taken place that morning.

MEANWHILE THERE WAS A *Kesselkommando*. The task of delivering soup to Block 10 fell to the five hospital blocks on a weekly roster. This week it was Block 9's turn and Hans was carrying a kettle together with Majzel, the quiet, gentle Belgian doctor whose wife was also in Block 10.

Most of the Pfleger were keen to get into Block 10. A lot of them had a girlfriend there, but even those who didn't know anyone wanted to spend a few seconds in the presence of women. That was why it was a crazy race from the kitchen to Block 10, because the four pairs who arrived first with their soup were allowed to deliver it there; the others had to take it to the men in Block 9.

On top of that, Hans and Majzel always picked out a heavy kettle. They felt that what a lot of the men did was a betrayal: wanting to see the women, they chose a small kettle to make it easier to get there first, in the process disadvantaging those same women by taking them too little soup.

But none of that mattered because with a different goal in mind than just a girlfriend, they were capable of a greater effort. And when Majzel – who was ten years older than Hans – couldn't keep up, they arranged the kettle on the poles so that Hans, who was strong and had tremendous endurance, was carrying most of the weight. That way they were generally first to arrive with their kettle.

Friedel was already waiting in the corridor.

The doorkeeper – the she-devil – had grown used to them and was a little less hostile.

Friedel smiled and put her hand on his chest. 'Silly boy, exerting yourself like that. Your heart's racing. That can't be good for you.'

'Be glad it's still beating.'

And immediately he felt the sharp pain of what he had seen that morning. He tried to conceal it, but she had already noticed. The women had seen all kinds of things from their windows too.

'How is it with the husbands of the girls here?'

'Miel Boekbinder is all right. Heini and Günther too, but a fellow called Geitenman is gone from Block 19.'

'My God, what am I going to tell her? She was pacing back and forth all morning completely beside herself. She was already so scared, because he's been in such a poor state. But she refuses to face up to it. I've even got a packet of bread here that she's given me for him.'

Hans thought it best to pretend everything was all right. Then, in a few days, they could tell her he was suddenly gone, transferred to another camp. No matter what, they mustn't let her know he'd been taken with today's selection.

'The poor girl, Samuel was at her this week too. She's been in a lot of pain and bled terribly. Can you get your hands on some cotton wool or cellulose? I can't possibly get enough here if they take as many samples as last week.'

Betty, Miel's wife, came up. She had two packets with her, one for Miel and one for Heini Spittel, from his wife.

'There aren't any letters in there, are there?' Hans asked. Getting caught with a packet of bread wasn't too bad, especially if you could show that it was from a woman for her own husband. But letters were different.

'There's a letter in my packet.'

'Get it out of there quickly, then. I'd rather hide it under my clothes.' Hans was starting to get nervous, because the doorkeeper had chased away almost all of the other men. He would have liked to discuss a few more things with Friedel, but arranging the packets always took a lot of time. Friedel could tell he was getting impatient. 'Just leave them. You're still their only chance of keeping in touch with their husbands.'

But before he could answer, the doorkeeper had spotted him, even though he'd hidden a little among the women.

'Have you gone mad?' she said, launching into her usual torrent of abuse. He wanted to spare himself the rest and gave Friedel a hasty kiss. But Friedel wouldn't accept that. She grabbed hold of him to at least say a proper goodbye.

Suddenly a door opened somewhere. A big fat woman appeared, one who looked like she'd come straight from a fish market, but without the clear, healthy complexion of a Dutch fisherwoman. Filthy, wispy tow-coloured hair, a round pasty face that formed a vile contrast to her scarlet-painted lips. She was heavily pregnant and looked grotesque in her poorly fitting uniform. *Was ist hier los, ihr Dreckhuren?*

It was a farce: this Nazi slut cursing his Friedel and the other women, who had given him bread they themselves had gone without to take to their husbands, as dirty whores. But the stick she was holding so casually was less farcical. That was why Hans kept himself hidden behind the women and slipped past the *Aufseherin* with the packets under his coat. He didn't breathe again until he was back in Block 9. That could have gone badly wrong.

IN BLOCK 9 THE soup kettles had already been distributed to the various rooms and wards. In the small rooms downstairs – 'small' meaning fifty patients per room – the sick men were allowed to stay in bed and the Pfleger took the soup around.

Janus, the Stubenältester, stood by the kettle to dish out the soup. One litre per person. Hans took the red tin bowls around. There were various patients who didn't want the soup. They ate too much from their packages. That meant soup to spare and Hans was able to fill another bowl with two litres and take it upstairs to give one of his fellow Dutchmen a little extra.

Upstairs it was organized differently. There the patients queued up in long lines with a bowl in their hands to receive their scoop from the kettle. Only the severely ill were allowed to stay in bed; the room orderlies brought them their food. Their lordships, the Pfleger, were too lazy to keep the ward clean and take food to the patients. Instead they had delegated the work to a few patients who were not quite so ill. Everyone was happy to be chosen for a job like that because it got you an extra litre of soup a day and meant you wouldn't be discharged from hospital and put in an outside Kommando. It was dangerous, of course. If the Lagerarzt came to pick out Mussulmen, the room orderlies had to hide in the attic or latrines.

When Hans entered the ward with his bowl of soup, people yelled out to him from all sides. 'Pfleger, give me some soup.' They pulled out the margarine they'd saved up and their bread from the previous day to buy the soup from Hans.

There were plenty of Pfleger who played along with things like that. The camp had a fully functioning black market. There were even fairly fixed prices. A litre of soup went for half a ration of bread or a whole ration of margarine. Some Pfleger and room orderlies exchanged five or more litres of soup for better quality food every day. There were even doctors who smuggled bowls of soup out of the window for some extra margarine. If caught, they would be kicked out of the Krankenbau, but they didn't let themselves get caught. Hans stayed aloof from all this buying and selling. It wasn't that he was so very virtuous; he didn't need it as badly.

Back downstairs, Zimmer called him to one side and pressed a packet in his hand. 'This week's package arrived today.'

Hans had to disappear quickly with his packet. The other Poles weren't allowed to see it; they would ridicule Zimmer for his kindness. He opened it in a corner of the nurses' room. It contained two apples, a piece of cake and a piece of bacon. He ate one of the apples and a bit of the cake immediately, hiding the rest under his mattress for Friedel. Then back to work: washing up bowls, sweeping the room. Kuczemba, the quartermaster, called. There was bread that had to be fetched and he needed a couple of sturdy lads: 120 loaves of bread – that was 170 kilos – in a carrying frame. Then another kettle Kommando: evening tea. On top of it all, a ticking-off from Paul: '*Du Dreckhund*, haven't you seen that tea's been spilt on the outside steps?' The outside steps were one of Hans's responsibilities. 'A job like that's an honour. The steps are our block's visiting card. You have to do your best to honour our block. Go and clean them up, fast. Give them a good scrub. Throw a couple of buckets of water over them, then with the broom. Yes, you know how.'

Hans certainly did. He ran through the corridors with the buckets of water like a man possessed and made as much fuss as possible to show everyone how hard he was working. That way he avoided one of his bosses reserving him for a subsequent job and was able, once he'd mopped the excess water off the steps, to slip into Ward 3 for a moment.

Ward 3 was the psychiatric department, where Eli Polak was the doctor. Eli was sitting in his corner at a table and staring drowsily into space. He was always a bit down and never seemed to have much energy. Although he was only thirty-five and physically robust, he often gave the impression of being a worn-out old man who wasn't up to anything any more.

It was understandable. Just three weeks after coming to Auschwitz he had heard that his wife and child – like all women with small children – had gone to Birkenau and 'up the chimney' immediately after arriving from Holland.

'You know,' he began telling Hans, 'I was standing in my line. My wife was loaded on to the lorry and I believe she fainted right then. I think somehow she'd caught on to what was going to happen.'

'Don't talk rubbish,' Hans snapped. He felt powerless to comfort Eli and in situations like this people often hide their embarrassment behind coarseness. 'What could she have noticed? And you know very well that they would have gone to the crematorium no matter what, whether she fainted or not.'

Then Walter started: 'In the name of the Führer, I, Walter, have been chosen as the Thousand-Year Reich's eternal delegate to the moon. I am the ruler over all stars and planets. My sister gave me three reichsmarks and that enabled me to maintain my economic control over the Hermann Göring Works. With our new weapons I have succeeded in tightening my hold on the universe and in the name of the trinity – Hitler, Goebbels and Göring – I am the viceroy of the great regions. My power knows no bounds. The Führer commands. The crazies in the ward will now hold a free election. Vote, vote, vote. You first, you dead loss, you sleepyhead, vote for the salvation of our Pan-Germanic empire. You damned democrat, will you wake up for once?'

He gave the poor imbecile who shared a bed with him a good shaking and hit him hard on the head. The man sat up and muttered something incomprehensible.

'Millions, millions are marching under our banners. Our blood has impregnated the eternal Goddess of Truth and she has given birth to the Führer, who will show us the way to the greatest realm of perfection. My children are the worms of blood and soil, their castings fertilize the earth that brings forth the corn with which we will withstand the blockade of England. You dirty, disbelieving dog. Get up. March in our ranks. *Judenblut spritzt vom Messer.* Everything is in our favour. March!'

And again he hit and kicked the poor bald-headed fool, who in his fear raised his hands to Walter in supplication. Eli had gone over and was trying to calm Walter down.

'That's right, Walter, the procession is tomorrow. You have to go to sleep today.'

'I shall never sleep, doctor. I am Siegfried, watching over the eternal maiden Brünhilde. She is slumbering in the tavern with the dragon, the Führer's father. I am the bodyguard of the brown blood. I am the banner of triumph. Hurrah, hurrah! I am Germania's son. Our columns are marching. March, march!'

He had leapt out of bed and was now marching back and forth across the room while roaring in ecstasy. All the madmen were in an uproar under Walter's rabble-rousing influence. Sitting on the sides of their beds, they were swinging their arms and legs. Pathetic idiots, otherwise completely calm, were slurring out inarticulate songs. A blissfully smiling hydrocephalic beat time on his bowl, while his cataract-covered eyes bulged in his horrifically swollen head.

Walter carried on marching, with Eli in hot pursuit.

'I am the boss. I am the apostle. I am the Führer of the whole madhouse.'

'That's right,' Hans said.

Then the roar of swearing drowned out the tumult: 'Herrgott Sakrament, verflucht noch mal—, what's going on here?' It was Paul, who had been alerted by the hullaballoo and had come to investigate.

It was soon over. He grabbed Walter by the scruff of the neck and sat him down on his bed. The whole meeting started to ebb away. 'Give him an injection, Polak. What are you standing there for, you good-for-nothings?'

Eli gave Walter his injection and things gradually calmed down. Paul pulled a chair up to the table.

'Listen, lads, you can't let things get out of hand so quickly. I've been in this madhouse for ten years now. You think I'm going to let myself be bullied around by a nutcase who thinks he's the Führer? The Führer himself hasn't cut me down to size yet.'

'Achtung!' rang through the building. Paul ran out of the room. Eli started cleaning his needle and Hans grabbed a broom and began sweeping diligently. *'Bewegung!'*

It was the SDG on his daily round. At first he'd ranted and raved, but recently he'd been mild. Zielina, the head doctor, had discovered his weak spot: now when the SDG went into the Blockältester's room, there was always a packet of cigarettes waiting for him. The Poles were happy to take turns offering one up out of their packages to avoid troublesome inspections. They could keep clothes in their beds, cook in the big stove now and then, and commit lots of other small transgressions. It wouldn't last much longer. The SDG would soon be transferred and a new one would come in his place. The camp leadership knew all too well that every guard, no matter how fierce, eventually comes to some level of accommodation with his prisoners. That's why the SDGs and all those who had a lot of contact with the Häftlinge were regularly transferred.

Three weeks later the new SDG showed up. He was a tall man with a blond moustache. He came to look around a little the first day and seemed very moderate. But a few days later he ordered all of the patients in the Polish ward out of bed. What was going on?

If it had been the Jews, they would have thought it was a selection, because they came there more or less every week to pick out the unfortunates. But the Poles?

Hans and the Stubenältester had to empty all of the beds and open all of the packages. All kinds of things appeared: clothes, shoes, old rags, mouldy bread and hundreds of other things. Everything was thrown on a pile. They were allowed to keep most of the food from the packages, but the SDG pocketed the tobacco and any special items like sardines or chocolate.

Meanwhile he carried out random checks, searching the patients and looking under the mattresses to make sure everything had been removed. Those who were wearing more than a single vest had to throw it on the pile and got a few slaps in return.

Zimmer scowled. He had received a magnificent woollen jumper and a pair of boots in the false bottom of a package. Now he was going to lose it all. It was already winter; one of these days he might be sent out in a Kommando.

The clothes and all the other gear were packed in blankets and the SDG said that it all had to go to the Blockältester's room. He had just started to count the bundles when a shot sounded outside in the street. The SDG walked over to the other side of the room to look out of the window and Hans seized his opportunity. With a bundle under each arm he slipped into the corridor.

When he came back, the SDG was standing over the bundles. Hans beat him to it: 'I've already taken one away.'

'Good, five more.'

Hans walked back and forth five more times and the SDG paid careful attention that nothing disappeared out of the bundles. When everything was in the Blockältester's room, he locked the door and took the key with him. He would come back later to pick it all up. But Zimmer's jumper and boots and the other choice items were already in the attic.

That evening Hans was rich. Zimmer had given him 250 grams of bacon when he'd returned his things. Just like that, in public, and the others whose possessions Hans had rescued didn't dare hold back either: bacon, sugar, apples, white bread and more. He was beaming as he stood near the Block 10 window to tell Friedel about his adventures.

'I'll bring you some of it tomorrow.'

'Keep enough for yourself.'

'I will.'

But he knew he would give most of it to her because, when he saw her at the window, he heard her coughing and she had already asked for cough medicine once before. He had asked her to take her temperature and she'd done it now for a couple of evenings: 37.3°C and 37.5°C under the arm. 'It's nothing,' she said.

But Hans was scared. He'd already spotted a new enemy: TB. He would fight against it. He would look after her. Sending food was all he could do, but he would do it, as long as he could. When he was lying in bed and thinking of how he had outsmarted the SDG, he felt a sense of satisfaction. A calmness he hadn't known for a long time came over him and he fell asleep with a smile on his face.

ONE MORNING HANS WAS called in to see the Blockältester: 'Van Dam, you have to go to quarantine.'

He was shocked and thought he was being kicked out of the Krankenbau again, but Zielina, who was also present, laughed and reassured him: 'They've got scarlet fever in quarantine and they need a doctor. For the time being, patients aren't allowed to be admitted from there to the Krankenbau. They're not allowed to go to the main outpatients to get their wounds dressed in the evenings either. That's why we have to send a doctor there to do the work on the spot.'

An hour later Hans arrived in quarantine. He was taken to the Blockältester, who met him with an ironic smile: 'So, this is the doctor, is it? That means you're the boss here now. Well, it will all be fine then.'

He led Hans to one of the rooms. In the corner a small cubicle was curtained off with blankets; behind them was an ordinary triple bunk. The Stubenältester slept on the ground floor with the clerk above him. The top bunk was for Hans.

The Stubenältester gave him a few tips on how to behave here in the quarantine block. Whatever else, he had to take it easy and not get wound up about anything.

If he had heeded that advice everything would have been all right. But right from the start, he began making conscientious and precise requests for all of the measures he deemed necessary. A dish containing disinfectant solution for people to wash their hands was needed at the door of every room. Everyone had to be subjected to a medical inspection every morning to identify new cases of scarlet fever as quickly as possible. There had to be an outpatients' clinic every evening. A small room needed to be cleared for the patients who, according to instructions, were not allowed to go to the Krankenbau, and for possible cases of scarlet fever. A few quarantined French doctors could help him. When Hans presented his list, the Blockältester answered with that same ironic smile: 'It will all be taken care of, Doctor.'

Hans was busy all day with these measures, none of which were carried out. There were no dishes for disinfectants. The Krankenbau chemist refused to supply medicine for non-hospital blocks. The Blockältester didn't have a spare room to set up a ward for the sick. After all, there were 1,200 people in his block. They were already sleeping three to a bunk.

But Hans felt that, more than just the impossibility of enacting his measures, it was deliberate obstruction. Heinrich, the Stubenältester whose cubicle Hans was sharing, even said as much. He wore a purple triangle next to the number on his breast, the symbol for Bible Students. Every evening there was a small meeting when all of the Bible Students would gather with Heinrich. There weren't many: five or six in all of Auschwitz. That hadn't always been the case, Heinrich told me.

Everyone in Germany who used the Bible to demonstrate the evil of the Nazi system and predict its downfall – the Jehovah's Witnesses – had been systematically picked up. The same had happened to those who believed in other prophecies, such as the divine message of the Great Pyramid or the prophecies of Nostradamus.

At one stage there were eight hundred of them together in Dachau.* The Lagerführer had them all line up on Roll Call Square. 'Who still believes in the truth of biblical predictions?' All hands were raised. The Sturmmänner picked out ten men, who were shot on the spot. Then again: 'Who still believes . . . ?' Again all hands were raised, again ten victims fell.

It went on like that, but with every round of that dance of death, more people were struck by doubt and fewer hands were raised, until finally only the 'converted' were left – though only after a hundred of the best had fallen.

They were sometimes wearying, the Bible Students, because no matter what you said, no matter what happened, they were always ready with a Bible quote, regardless of how irrelevant it was. But they were honest, they had your best wishes at heart, and they knew what was what in the camp.

'Be careful, son,' Heinrich warned Hans. 'Don't make things too difficult for them with all your precautions. Before you know it you'll be in deep trouble.'

A few days later the SS doctor came. He kicked up an enormous fuss and gave Hans a dressing-down because all kinds of measures to prevent an epidemic hadn't been taken. Stupidly, Hans was too sporting to answer that he had ordered the measures but hadn't received any cooperation from the Blockältester. Now the Blockältester was thwarting him even more, because he thought Hans's silence had been motivated by fear.

The only one to help Hans at all was a young Czech colleague. He had been put in the camp as a homosexual, but

---

* Dachau, established in 1933, was the first Nazi concentration camp and became a model for all others. Initially described as being for political prisoners, it was developed on the site of an abandoned munitions factory ten miles north-west of Munich.

because he wasn't Jewish and, as a Czech, could speak Polish with the Blockältester, he was sometimes able to get things done. Ivar became a good friend. He told Hans how he had got his pink triangle.

'A party member in Prague had an old debt to me. When I insisted on payment, he set the Gestapo on me with a statement about how he had supposedly caught me performing homosexual acts. Anyway, Hans, you know how German justice works. I never admitted anything and nothing was ever proven. But a single Nazi witness counts more than the best alibi. I could have proven I wasn't in Prague at all on the day of the "crime", but they don't give you a chance.'

The next day Hans experienced German justice first-hand. He was at work upstairs in a corner of the attic – where ten unfortunate patients were bedded down on a thin, filthy layer of straw – when the gong for the roll call sounded. As it took at least half an hour from the gong until the arrival of the SS man, the Stubenältester hurried down to Hans's room to let them know to take him into account. But when Hans went downstairs a little later, the count had still been wrong. The Blockältester had been called in and the moment Hans entered the room he started to abuse him, shouting 'Cholera . . .' and a hundred other Polish swear words.

Hans tried to clarify the situation and apologize, but the Blockältester grew more and more agitated and then, without warning, punched him several times hard in the face. Blood gushed from Hans's nose and his glasses lay shattered on the floor.

But worse than the smashed glasses and his crooked nose – broken by the first blow – he was now a lost cause in quarantine. All of the Stubenälteste and their assistants, the clerks and orderlies, were laughing at him. Nobody listened to him any more.

That evening Hans discussed it with Krutkov, one of the few Russians who spoke a little German. He had been the head of a *Kolkhoz*, a collective farm with some 2,500 workers. When the Germans arrived they had all refused to continue working. A lot of them were shot dead on the spot. He was here in the camp with a couple of hundred of his people.

They all had black triangles: antisocial, work-shy. Imagine, people who had worked like horses, who had turned their village with its hovels and muddy fields into a fabulous vast farm, who knew better than anyone in the whole world the meaning of community, a community of workers and peasants, and working for that community, labelled here as antisocial.

What did it matter what kind of triangle you wore here, how you were appreciated here?

'Look around at all the people imprisoned here,' the Russian continued. 'Most of them are Polish, with those red triangles with a P on them – political prisoners – but I guarantee you that ninety per cent are black marketeers, or that their political activities were at most stupid statements they made when drunk. The Germans with a red triangle are more likely to be real political prisoners. Some of them have been imprisoned for ten years, but there aren't many here. Most of them are already dead anyway. Then you've got the Russians, who, as I said, mostly have black triangles. In reality they're actual political prisoners, because their refusal to work was a political act. The worst scum are often the greens. If the triangle is pointing up, they're *Berufsverbrecher*, professional criminals. Pointing down means an occasional criminal. In the camps they get to lord it over the others. As Lagerälteste, some of them have the deaths of hundreds of fellow prisoners on their consciences. But that, too, is all so random. I knew a German from Cologne who scattered political pamphlets from a plane in 1936 – anti-Nazi of course. He was caught and they proved that he had accepted money from an illegal organization to pay for the printing costs. They gave him a green triangle – as a criminal. If he'd printed them at his own expense, it would have been a red triangle.'

Evening had fallen in the meantime and Hans needed to check upstairs for a moment. It was a large attic, sleeping three hundred, almost all of whom were lying directly on the cement floor. They were all Jews. A few days earlier a Jew had been caught urinating in a food bowl. Sometimes they weren't allowed outside for half a day and this fellow had a bladder complaint and couldn't hold it in that long. That was why a friend from a work block had brought a separate bowl for him, but those excuses weren't accepted. They beat him black and blue and, as always, if one Jew had done something wrong, all of the Jews were swine. The Blockältester had seized the opportunity to move them all up to the attic, simultaneously making room on the lower floors for the Poles, who no longer had to sleep more than two a bunk.

The attic was a ghastly shambles: an unpolished cement floor, a leaky roof and two small windows to provide fresh air to three hundred people. The men had to lie on the floor in their linen uniforms with one blanket for two men. In the daytime they jostled for a seat on a couple of rafters or had to stand because there were neither chairs nor tables. They had been living like this for five weeks now, as none of them were allowed to leave the block because of the scarlet fever.

All the sick prisoners from the entire block were crammed into a corner that was partitioned off with walls made of board. The filth was appalling. Still, there was an advantage to this, as they weren't being trampled by the hundreds of others shuffling back and forth across the attic. But if a Pole or a Russian fell ill, all kinds of difficulties arose. Of course the patient would rather stay in bed downstairs than move up to the filthy sick corner, but sick prisoners weren't allowed to stay in the rooms because of the risk of contagion. After all, you could never say in advance that a particular case of angina with a forty-degree fever was definitely scarlet fever. The patient would scheme a little with the Stubenältester, who in turn spoke to the Blockältester, and then, regardless of what Hans had ordered, the sick prisoner stayed just where he was. It was clear that he didn't belong there from a hygiene point of view, but from the sick man's perspective it was very understandable. In the attic he wouldn't get any rest or fresh air, and would receive no more treatment than downstairs.

There were almost no bandages and even less medicine. For two days Hans was given thirty aspirins for 1,200 people. And with all these prisoners jammed in together, many of them fell ill. It had taken quite a lot of effort for him to get those thirty tablets. He'd had to go to Dering, the head of the Krankenbau.

The patients were lying in their corner. Several of them had a high fever and hadn't been able to eat for days because their throats were so sore. There was a special kitchen for restricted diets attached to the Krankenbau, but to use it you needed a note from the Blockältester, who didn't have time for things like that. Still, it was very stupid of Hans to complain to Dering the following day about the conditions and about the Blockältester hitting him.

At first Dering kicked up an enormous fuss, saying that a Blockältester hitting a doctor was a disgrace and an insult to the whole Krankenbau, but then the Blockältester himself joined them. They talked a little in Polish and Dering calmed down. He would investigate the matter further.

An hour later he sent for Hans again. 'I see that you don't have enough tact for this situation. You're going back to the block where you first worked.'

WHEN HE GOT TO Block 9 they had already heard about it. Zielina, the head doctor, ridiculed him for having let them ride roughshod over him like that.

Hans was sent to Dr Valentin, the head of outpatients: 'You were lucky. Dering could have reported you to the Lager-arzt immediately, then you would have gone straight into a coal mine. Oh well, whether they get rid of you today or next week . . .'

'What do you mean?'

'Ah, dopey doesn't know anything about it, of course. Haven't you heard of the Pfleger cutback – sorry, Pfleger transport?'

'What's that?'

'Next week sixty Pfleger have to go to Buna. They say they're setting up a new hospital there.'

'That's not so bad,' Hans ventured.

'Boy, are you naive,' Valentin mocked. 'They say they're going to Buna as Pfleger and doctors, but you'll see that not one of them ends up in the infirmary, unless it's as a patient who's been worked half to death!'

Things didn't look good. Hans had only been in the camp for a relatively short period. He would be sent away before others who had been here much longer. That evening he discussed the situation with Eli Polak and Klempfner, a Czech doctor from the upstairs ward. Klempfner had already spent four years in various camps and knew the ins and outs.

'Don't worry,' he said. 'Ten people have to go from this block, but you'll see, you won't be one of them.'

'How do you know that?'

'Zielina is making the list and he thinks highly of both of you.'

'Well, I'm sure he doesn't think highly of me any more after the way I made a fool of myself in quarantine,' Hans sneered.

'Don't say that. You didn't make a fool of yourself at all. You were much too fair, of course, and you have far too many scruples. You wanted to stick up for the sick and that rubbed his lordship the Blockältester the wrong way because it was too much work. But Zielina's a fine fellow and he's well aware of what's really going on. You mustn't lump all Poles into the same basket.'

Klempfner was right. A few days later Zielina let Hans know unofficially that everything would be all right. He was going to keep him and Eli because he thought the Dutch were decent types. Still, there were victims among the Dutch prisoners all the same: Tony Haaksteen and Gerard van Wijk. Zielina's not keeping them was understandable. They weren't doctors and they had been in the camp the shortest. Tony wasn't popular; he was nervous, yelled at the patients terribly and got into regular conflicts with the other Pfleger. But Hans thought it was an awful shame about Gerard. He was a gentle, intelligent lad. He was fairly weak and had already coughed up blood a couple of times.

'What are they going to do with us?' Gerard asked.

'Well, you're going to that new hospital there.' Hans didn't actually believe this, but what use was there in upsetting the poor fellow even more?

The Pfleger left on a Wednesday. They had washed and they were wearing 'new' clothes. That was a bad sign because Pfleger or doctors who were really going to keep working in their 'profession' didn't need to swap their clean suits for rags.

On Thursday afternoon, when Hans arrived with a soup kettle, he found the women in Block 10 in something of a panic. Professor Samuel had been taken away from his work that morning on orders of *Standortarzt* Wirths, the SS doctor in charge of all Lagerärzte in the Auschwitz area. The rumour was that he had to go to Birkenau to find new female subjects for their experiments. The girls were convinced that the block's current residents would then be put in outside Kommandos. They had submitted to the experiments and would end up dying like dogs in a gravel pit anyway.

Hans had heard a different story and reassured Friedel: 'For the last couple of weeks there's been a conflict between Samuel and Clauberg. It seems that Samuel wanted to protect the staff more and asked the Standortarzt if forty "deserving" women who worked in the block, and were already on his list, could be exempted from the Clauberg experiments.'

'It's possible,' Friedel said. 'There's so much conniving going on here. Yesterday Brewda had an enormous quarrel with Sylvia, Clauberg's assistant, a foul girl. She already said a month ago that the staff were all going to be done too. After characters like that have been in a camp for two or three years and obtained some power, they forget they're prisoners themselves too.'

'Who's Brewda?' Hans asked.

'Our current Blockälteste. She's a doctor, but she sabotages the experiments when she can.'

Hans went to Block 9 to hear what Klempfner thought.

'If Samuel gets shot at Birkenau, Brewda won't stay on as Blockälteste either,' he said.

'Then they'll probably use the staff for experiments too?'

'Probably, but is that so bad? It's better than the first interpretation, that Samuel's gone to get new guinea pigs. They're better off getting an injection than being sent to Birkenau. Those experiments aren't that terrible. Sure, those Greek girls were horribly mauled, but among Clauberg's subjects there's only been the sporadic death and a few cases of peritonitis, and we don't actually know the percentage of infertility.'

Hans agreed with Klempfner inasmuch as anything was better than Birkenau. But he couldn't go along with his opinion that the experiments 'weren't that terrible.'

'Even if they only harm a single hair on those women's heads, it's still as bad a crime as a major operation, because the nature of the crime is not determined by the seriousness of the experiment, but by the compulsion under which it is carried out. Anyway, if the experiment wasn't serious they wouldn't have to force prisoners to take part. If I want to set up an innocent study, I can find people who are willing to volunteer to take part at an ordinary clinic. Their using prisoners is proof in itself that something's wrong. Economically, capitalist progress often comes at the expense of workers. But IG Farben* wanting progress at the expense of our women's bodies, that's something that not even modern capitalism would approve in any country except Germany.'

---

* A German chemical and pharmaceutical conglomerate, once the largest company in Europe, which from 1933 worked closely with the Nazis.

'You're right there,' Klempfner replied. 'It really is remarkable that the fascists, when protecting big business, whose tool they are, so often resort to pre-capitalist means.'

'How's that?'

'Take their power structure. It's pure feudalism. Here in the camp you see it in a stylized version. A camp is a kind of duchy. The Lagerältester is the liege lord by the grace of the SS. He exercises his power by granting privileges. The Blockälteste are the counts; their position as petty potentates allows them to "organize." Their staff are like minor nobility terrorizing the land. Take our block's doorkeeper, for example.

'In an ordinary hospital the doorkeeper is paid a wage for the work he does. Here he's a person of power. From each visitor he allows in, he demands a cigarette or more. Each service he carries out for a patient has to be paid for. That's how he looks after number one. Only the masses, who don't have a position of power, die on a litre of soup and a ration of bread a day. It's the crudest possible connection between power and rights. Completely undemocratic, feudal.'

When Hans went to go downstairs, someone called out to him.

'Hello, Van Dam, are you here too?'

Lying on a middle bunk was a tall young man, skin and bones and too weak to raise himself up in bed.

'Lex, how long have you been here?'

It was Lex van Weren, the jazz trumpet player Hans used to play with now and then.

'Did you know that Jack de Vries is here too?' Lex asked. 'He's working in one of the mining Kommandos. And Maurice van Kleef. He's in the Birkenau orchestra.'

'How did he manage that?'

'In Birkenau Jews are allowed in the orchestra. It's got a load of Dutch celebrities in it. Johnny and Jones, and Han Hollander too.'

They reminisced and Lex told him what it had been like in Jawischowitz,* in the coal mine: 'With two of you, you have to fill forty carts a day. That's the same amount as the civilian workers, the professional miners. But they know the trade, and if you don't know how to use a pickaxe you don't get a single coal loose. That means a beating. The first day we only filled five carts. That was so little it counted as sabotage. But believe me, it's the most you can manage. For punishment they put us in the *Stehbunker* that night. That's a cellar that's too low to stand up in, but you can't lie down either, because there's a few centimetres of water on the floor. So you spend the whole night bent over in the pitch black. You can understand how rotten you feel the next day and that you're hardly able to work at all. Then you get another beating and different punishments. No one can bear treatment like that. The civilians get normal food with a miner's supplement. We have to live off a ration of bread and a litre of soup. When the miners get back home they have some peace and quiet; they go to sleep or spend an hour in the pub. But we have roll call with knee bends, flat on your stomach in the mud – 'stand up, lie down, stand up' – and so on for hours on end. Then into your bunk, eight men on one wide wooden bed, cold, no rest. At four in the morning they wake you up and it starts all over again.

'No chance to be sick. Diarrhoea? *Get to work!* Fever? *Get to work!* Until you're this close to death. And the risks underground! They don't take any safety measures at all in

* Jawischowitz was an Auschwitz sub-camp between 1942 and 1945.

the galleries where prisoners work. Accidents all the time. Stupid, because their own production suffers as a result. We arrived half a year ago with a thousand people from Holland. They picked out three hundred men. The rest were probably gassed. We, the three hundred, were sent to the mines. About fifteen are alive now. I was lucky: one day the Lagerältester came traipsing up with an old French horn. How he got it, I don't know, but he asked me if it was true that I could play the trumpet. Then I played for the Rapportführer: "Silent Night". It was Christmas and all evening they wanted to hear the same thing over and over again. "Silent Night". I had to think of the night in the Stehbunker. Anyhow, then they made me a room orderly. I didn't need to go down the mine any more. I had to clean the barracks, fetch bread and do jobs like that. Now and then I played something for the big shots, then I got something extra to eat. Yes, you need a special stroke of luck here, otherwise they grind you down without mercy.'

'Indeed, gentlemen, indeed.' An affected, posh voice came from the top bunk.

'What kind of joker are you?' Hans asked.

'My name's Menko and it's true, I am a joker, but I've been playing jokes on the SS. I've been imprisoned since January 1941.'

Hans gave him a disbelieving look. 'Transports to Poland hadn't even started in January '41.'

'No, I was picked up with the Geuzen.* At the trial in '41, they sentenced me to death.'

'What are you doing here then?' another Dutchman interjected.

---

* The Geuzen was a Dutch anti-German resistance group.

'You, Sir, are another joker, but a damned feeble one. Nonetheless, I shall answer you. I have been through at least a dozen prisons and just as many camps. But as is so often the case with people who have been sentenced to death, you wait for your execution and it doesn't come. The most extreme is Buchenwald. There are hundreds of prisoners there who have been sentenced to death. Now and then they send a transport to *Nebellager* Natzweiler.'

'Why is it called a *Nebellager*?'

'Patience, gentlemen. In Natzweiler the executions take place "*zwischen Nacht und Nebel*", at the crack of dawn. That has something mystical and heathen about it. The *Übermensch* is full of these atavistic tendencies. Anyway, I was supposed to go on a transport to Natzweiler. But in Buchenwald the political prisoners were in the key positions – in the administration and so on. When a transport of tradesmen had to be sent to Sachsenhausen – which used to be called Oranienburg – they put as many of the people with death sentences on it as they could. After a lot of hither and thither I ended up in Auschwitz and I'm just fine here. With my Mussulman body, I was put down for a selection last week. The poor sods were picked up the next day, but I pulled another fast one. I'm not registered here in the card system as a Jew, but as a *Schutzhäftling*. I'm not part of the nameless army of millions that will go up in smoke here. There are documents about me; I'm involved in a legal process. I'm only allowed to die by execution and they're not executing me here in Auschwitz either. They're counting on me, as a Jew, dropping dead by myself.'

'There are more cases like that,' Hans told him. 'In Birkenau there's a fellow called Boas, a French teacher from Amsterdam. He had got a job as an interpreter with the workers on the

Channel coast, using forged papers. He and two friends were caught. Espionage trial. All sentenced to death. The friends, who had kept quiet about being Jewish, were put before the firing squad immediately, but Boas admitted to being a Jew.

'The SS officer told him: "You, Jew, you're going to Auschwitz. You'll end up begging for death, it will be so bad." Now Boas is in a good Kommando and if his luck holds, he'll come through it alive, by virtue of being a Jew.'

WITH SO MANY PFLEGER GONE, Hans was very busy, lugging things around from the morning gong until night, when the gong rang for bed. Early in the morning, immediately after getting up, there was the kettle Kommando: fetching tea, bringing it round, washing plates and making the bed. Meanwhile the Stubenältester had already started mopping the ward, as everything had to be clean by eight o'clock at the latest. That was when the SDG did his inspection.

After that there were all kinds of jobs to do inside the block. One day the corridor needed to be thoroughly cleaned and they were at it all morning with buckets of water, scrubbing and mopping; the next day it was helping the Scheissmeister by scraping out the latrines. One day it was unloading coal, another delousing the upstairs ward when lice had been spotted again. It was hard work, because in the whole block with its four hundred patients there were only thirty Pfleger and half of those were prominents: Poles, Reich Germans and 'low numbers' whose only concern was 'organizing' as much food as possible. That left just ten of them at most for the heavy work. Then came the midday soup, with a repeat of the morning rituals.

One day, after the soup, a messenger came from Block 21: transport Kommando. Thirty of them turned out, this time without a wagon. They were taken to the old crematorium, two hundred metres from the camp. It was no longer in use.

Now that all of the extermination was being done in Birkenau, there were only 'normal' deaths in Auschwitz and the few bodies were taken to the Birkenau furnaces on corpse wagons in the evenings.

In one of the rooms in the crematorium there were enormous stacks of tins: the urns of the Poles whose bodies had been burnt there. In contrast to Jews, 'Aryans' were cremated individually. A clay number was placed on each body and the ashes were put in a tin urn. The family received a death notice and could claim the urn. But, over the years, forty thousand urns had been left behind and now had to be moved to another room.

The men formed a long chain right through the cellars where the three large furnaces were and tossed the urns to each other as if they were cheeses or loaves of bread. Never before had so many dead passed through Hans's hands as in those few hours. The tins were rusty and if you dropped one, it broke open. That didn't matter: one of the lads had a broom and swept all the ashes into a pile. Who would ever request them now?

They arrived back in the block just before roll call, which only took a few minutes. They lined up, the SDG came, the Blockältester reported: 'Block 9 with thirty-one Pfleger lined up for roll call, none sick.' Then the SDG gave a wave and they were dismissed.

After roll call, Hans had to go upstairs to help Dr Valentin in outpatients. There was an enormous racket on the stairs. Zielina, as nervous as ever, had exploded in fury at a man who had tried to go to the latrines without any wooden sandals – barefoot, in other words – which was strictly forbidden. In his rage, he had hit the man in the face, but Zielina had a good heart and when the man burst into tears, he was even more upset than his victim. He raced downstairs and came back with a piece of bread – bread from home, out of his own package – which he gave to the man. The years in concentration camps had left their mark on Zielina, but they hadn't ruined him.

In outpatients Valentin was already ranting. He was a half-Jew who had been a doctor in the navy. Not a bad man, but a real Prussian. He would roar at anyone at the slightest provocation, but if you responded by looking around in bewilderment, he'd burst out laughing.

'So, look who else is here. Dutch barns must be full of babies, the way you all leave the door open. You were naive enough to think the Pfleger were going to the Krankenbau in Buna, remember? I just got news. They're all in the outside Kommando. So . . .' And then to the various doctors who had come to assist with the daily dressings: 'Come with me for a moment. I'll show you something.'

He led them to the bed of a patient who had terrible hiccups. 'He's been like this for three days,' Valentin recounted, 'and nothing I've done has helped. He has also had a high fever, up to forty degrees in the evenings for a week now. What do you think it is?'

They thought for a while.

Hans suggested: 'It could be meningitis. That often leads to symptoms of nervous irritation like hiccups.'

'Wrong,' Valentin said. 'It's typhus without the rash, not infrequent. He's from an infected camp.'

'Isn't it dangerous to keep him here on the ward?' one of the Frenchmen asked.

'Not at all, we don't have any lice at the moment and he's been thoroughly decontaminated. Anyway, there's no question of my reporting him. It wouldn't be the first time a whole block went to the gas chamber after a case of typhus. Make sure you keep your mouths shut.'

Then the outpatients parade began. The patients came in through the back door with their vests up or completely removed, depending on what needed dressing. Their wounds were often awful – boils and abscesses – and the worst thing was that they all had to be dressed with paper. After half an hour, outpatients stank so badly it was almost unbearable. On top of that, everything was dirty and greasy from Mitigal, the oil they used for scabies and one of the few medicaments in stock.

Suddenly Eli stormed in: 'Did you know Kalker's dead?'

They were shocked.

'Didn't it help?' Hans asked.

'No, it was too expensive. He needed a lot more sulpha, but none of the Dutchmen had enough supplies to pay for it all.'

They discussed it for a while until Valentin erupted: 'Keep your chit-chat for teatime. Just like home; I always had to take care of everything there too, but I'm not doing it any more.'

The Blockältester came in. He needed four men and took Hans with him. They went to Block 21 with the SDG and picked up an examination chair that had to be taken to the brothel. There was a crowd out the front with a long line of Reich Germans and Poles. Jews were not admitted.

Business had not yet started and upstairs the ladies were clumped together arguing with the supervising doctor and nurse. The doctor had to be present when the men came in and paid their reichsmark – reichsmarks they earned as a bonus from their work. He gave them an injection and a stamp on the left arm and when they came out again a quarter of an hour later, they got another injection and a stamp on the right arm. At the exit there was an SS guard who checked to make sure they had both stamps. This was to prevent the spread of venereal disease.

One of the ladies gave Hans a tug on the ear and said, 'What are you doing here, boy? You're not allowed in here.'

'Just do your job,' Hans sneered, 'I'm here for mine.'

'Yeah, sure,' she replied. '*Arbeit macht frei . . . Krematorium drei!*'

Back in the block it was already late in the evening and, as always, Hans had to sweep the room before he could go to sleep. But before he'd finished, the Blockältester came and started ranting about the light still being on even though the evening gong had long since rung. Quickly, Hans undressed and went to bed.

It had been a long day – sixteen hours without a break! And what for? For a long time until he finally fell asleep the madam's parody echoed in his ear: 'Work sets you free . . . Crematorium three!'

TIME PASSED. SOMETIMES THINGS went a little better for Hans and Friedel, sometimes worse. The selections returned regularly and there were always more friends for them to mourn. And they weren't always the severely ill or those who had been worked half to death.

People with jobs in the camp weren't safe. Auschwitz workers were constantly being put on transports to other camps. People who worked in the better Kommandos weren't safe from the selections either. And once they'd been put on a transport they generally didn't last long. Who could survive working in the mines? Who was capable of dredging gravel out of the river fourteen hours a day, often up to the waist in the water? Who could bear the blows and resist the infections?

Spring came, and with it the sparse birds. Birds that ventured to this cold corner of Silesia, braving the bleak weather on the north side of the Beskid Mountains. But spring came and the sun had life energy and that energy penetrated everything. No barbed wire, no wall, no SS could stop the sun.

With the sun, new life came into those who were doomed to die, and new hope unfurled in their hearts, like fresh green leaves released from tiny buds to receive the rays of new light. The air was mild and moist, the sky was bright blue, and hearts beat faster as they tasted spring. It was as if their blood had become more liquid and was flowing through their veins with renewed zeal. As if their souls were trembling in their bodies, together with the air, which was shimmering over the green fields. A tension came into them, as old as the history of mankind, but new again now, after this soul-chilling winter.

And as Hans and Friedel stood at the windows of their blocks looking at each other, the unattainable, and at the mountains, the unreachable, they felt like Adam and Eve longing for a paradise – not one they had been driven out of, but one they had never known. A deep sigh and their souls left their shackled bodies and floated off into the hazy distance, and for a moment the camp no longer existed. The horrors had disappeared, along with the wire and the wall. Their souls, united with each other and the whole cosmos, billowed away over the river and marshes to that glorious blue land of promise on the horizon. Then they looked at each other again, and in them rose that one word, which they did not speak out loud, yet heard in the other's voice across the metres that separated them: 'When?'

When would their longing for freedom, for being able to love each other in freedom, be fulfilled? Freedom together seemed inconceivable, and a gruesome fear passed through them when they thought of the death camp in which they were imprisoned. And when their thoughts, no longer carried aloft by fantasy, returned to reality, her fingers curled tightly around the wire and his hands gripped the window frame, as if they were both straining themselves to the limit to break something, something that was blocking them off from everything.

Then they sighed again, but this sigh was very different. Now it was full of regret and grieving for the dreamland they were convinced would never be theirs.

That evening Hans felt ill. He went straight to bed after roll call and asked one of the lads to fetch a thermometer from outpatients. His temperature was only up a little bit and he realized he was just suffering from the tensions spring had set off in him.

But why not take a few days' rest? Paul wouldn't give him any trouble. Paul was in love. For weeks now, he had been sitting at the window of his room watching out for that one small woman who was so friendly to a kind older man. Because Paul really had become kind-hearted since falling in love with a Dutch Jew from the women's block. He no longer harassed the Pfleger and he had stopped swearing at them. It was an honest love on Paul's part – an honest, compassionate love.

He and Hans had formed an alliance. Hans took Paul's notes and packages to Block 10; Paul let Hans take it easy whenever he could. That was why Hans was able to stay sick for a couple of days without worrying; nobody would call him to account. He sent a note to Friedel with the kettle carriers, telling her that he was taking a couple of days' rest and she needn't worry. The next day he got a long letter in reply:

Dear sweetheart,

I'm glad you're getting some rest now and not driving yourself into the ground so much. I can get by without seeing each other for a couple of days and without you taking care of extra food for me.

Yesterday was a special day. I had been asking the Blockälteste for a long time and finally I was allowed to go with the herb Kommando. At eight a.m. we left the camp. We walked a long way and also came close to Birkenau. I saw Lotte Spatel there and the other girls who left our block last month. With some of them, the experiments had been completed. With others, they had failed. There were also some, like Lotte and the French Communists, who had refused to submit to the experiments.

Altogether seventy of them were put on the transport three weeks ago. It's awful to see those women in Birkenau. How they have changed. Heads shaved completely bald and with bare feet, nothing but a piece of sacking to cover their bodies, bound together with a cord. You know, Hans, they're not women any more, they're creatures, asexual creatures. Our girls still look fairly good, but how long will that last?

I spoke to Lotte for a moment. She quickly scrawled out a few words for her husband, Heini, but the overseer came up right away and gave her a clip. Then she went back to lugging bricks. You're right – if I got sent to Birkenau I wouldn't last long. I'm already coughing so much as it is.

It was a beautiful day. We looked for herbs in the woods. Chamomile and all kinds of other herbs. They use them to make *Heilkräutertee*. It was joyous: you could feel spring in every stem, in every blossom. Here in the camp everything is as dry and dead as ever, but the woods have already come back to life with birds and with new shoots on the branches of the trees.

We came back late in the afternoon. I was dead on my feet. I wasn't used to it.

The evening was horrific. Yesterday afternoon there was a *Standgericht*. Three cars arrived with 'judges'. In a nearby village they'd picked up more than three hundred Poles – the entire population. Only two were acquitted. The executions were in the evening.

We could hear it all perfectly. It was in the inner courtyard of Block 11, right next door. On that side our windows are boarded over and the Blockälteste made sure we didn't look through the chinks, because then they would have been sure to shoot at the windows.

The mood in our block was worse than ever. The room orderlies were raging and the clerk was lashing out constantly. They're all women – Slovakians – who spent a long time in Birkenau. Of course, things were hideous for them there, but now they think they have to make it hideous for us too. "If you'd been in Birkenau, you'd be long dead by now," they say, and that's why we have to undergo their harsh treatment now. Always that system of taking it out on others.

At seven, the shooting started. We were so nervous and it was so muggy and close in the room and every time a volley sounded it went right through us. It was as if it was going to be our turn next, we felt it that intensely.

First the order to fire, then a volley, then the bodies being dragged away. And it kept on going like that. And then the cries of the victims. A girl begging for mercy because she was still so young and so desperate to live. The men, who shouted out all kinds of patriotic slogans like '*Hitler verrecke!*' and '*Es lebe Polen!*'

The mood in our block has been so bad lately anyway. It must be because it's spring and being shut up in a gloomy room with some two hundred women, waiting until you're called for. And they call for so many of us. I can tell you some more about it now, as I know more or less what they're doing. You know about Schumann's experiments, don't you? He took Greek girls aged about seventeen and put them in an electric ultra-shortwave field, with one plate on their abdomen and another on their buttocks. It burnt the ovaries, but the electric current caused horrific wounds and the girls suffered enormous pain. Inasmuch as they healed, they were then operated on to see how the internal organs, especially the ovaries, had been burnt.

Slawa explained to me that this method is madness: they want to find an easy sterilization technique so that they can sterilize all kinds of people, like Poles, Russians and, if it suits them, maybe the Dutch too. But this way the women are not only sterile, they're castrated as well.

After the experiments were completed, they sent the girls to Birkenau. A month later, they brought them back for operations to see how it had worked. Schumann removed their ovaries to see what kind of condition they were in. Imagine it: nine abdominal operations in two-and-a-quarter hours. They didn't sterilize the instruments once between operations.

Then there are Samuel's experiments, which you know more about than I do. He's been at almost all of the women, some four hundred. They suffer dreadful pain. Anyway, you know that. It can't be true that he just removes a small piece of mucosa because it gives the women terrible trouble and they all need stitches.

When Schumann failed, Professor Clauberg came. He's apparently a well-known gynaecologist from Kattowitz. He injects a white, cement-like liquid into the women's uteruses and X-rays them at the same time. Clauberg says it's to find a replacement for Lipiodol. You see, in Germany they don't have any iodine to use as a contrast medium for X-ray photography. I don't know if that's entirely true. It could also be intended as some kind of sterilization technique.

Well, that's enough nastiness for one day. Don't be angry at me for not writing more pleasant things, but you were so keen to know everything exactly.

Bye, sweetheart, have a good rest . . .

And then a hundred more sweet words and wishes followed, stirring that great longing in Hans once again. He leapt out of bed and got dressed. It was half past three and the soup kettle had already been delivered, but he was desperate to see her, to speak to her for a moment, to comfort her and try to build up her spirits.

The door to Block 10 was open. The doorkeeper didn't seem to be around. Hans hesitated for a second and then, for the first time, went in just like that, without a kettle. In the corridor he saw a Dutchwoman, who went to get Friedel for him. But no sooner were they standing opposite each other than the doorkeeper came sailing out of one of the rooms and started yelling. Where did he get the nerve, in the middle of the day! If she'd kept herself under control a little, it would have all turned out all right, but she screamed so much that things had to go wrong. Hans started getting nervous. Suddenly Goebel was there in front of him.

Dr Goebel was a puny little chap in civilian riding breeches, which are not flattering at all if you have spindly legs. With his light sports jacket he gave the impression of a low-level civil servant who's picked up something at a clearance sale. But the women hated and feared him.

Clauberg could be reasonable sometimes and would often spare a woman if she had some reason to request not being injected. But two weeks ago Goebel had appeared and seemed to have come to Block 10 as some kind of supervisor. He stuck his nose into everything and mercilessly forced all of the women to participate in the experiments. He wasn't a medical doctor, but a chemist from IG Farben, the company that funded the experiments and had a financial interest in the new liquids. Goebel was coarse and sarcastic and had the meanness that was typical of all these people who had never learnt to lead and suddenly had power over others.

'Does the gentleman think it's a casino here perhaps?'

Hans was not usually shy of an excuse. But in this instant hatred flared inside him. He found it so difficult to suppress and felt such an urge to kick the pipsqueak to the ground that he was only able to stammer out a few incomprehensible syllables.

'We'll sort it out,' said the mighty one, noting down the number Hans wore on his left breast. Hans slunk off and spoke to no one about his adventure. The next morning Paul came up to him.

'Son, what's going on? Your number came in from the Schreibstube, you have to go up to the front of the camp.'

'To the front of the camp' meant to the gate, where the Rapportführer had his office. He had to wait in the small hallway of the Blockführerstube.

Kaduk, the Rapportführer, addressed Hans: '150822.'

'*Zum Befehl,*' he responded. At your command.

'*Überstellung Strafkommando Birkenau.*'

He was being sent to the punishment detail at Birkenau.

Hans's head was still spinning when the SS Sturmmann who was going to escort him to the punishment detail arrived. His legs felt like lead and he found it hard to keep up. Midway between Auschwitz and Birkenau was the large viaduct over the railway yards of the town of Auschwitz. From there, the road followed a branch of the railway line and after about half a kilometre, they reached Birkenau. The tracks and road entered the camp through a gate in the main building and formed the midline of an enormous sea of barracks.

Eight or ten side roads ran off the railway line at right angles and were flanked on both sides by rows of thirty-five to forty barracks. The left side of the camp was called *FKL*, the *Frauenkonzentrationslager*. On the right was the *Arbeitslager Birkenau*. So called because, although it was a labour camp by name, the conditions were even worse here than in the women's concentration camp. This was where the crematoria were – four in number.

Roll calls and inspections, food distribution and Kommandos would have been impossible to organize if they had allowed all two hundred thousand prisoners free access to the entire grounds of Birkenau. That was why each side street, with its rows of barracks, formed a distinct camp. All of these camps had their own number or letter and were cut off from each other by barbed wire. As a consequence, it was possible for a husband and wife, or mother and daughter, to live in

Birkenau for months without knowing of each other's existence, as all the camps were kept strictly separate and the only communication was between adjoining camps and poor.

Still, contact between men and women, although highly dangerous, was more extensive here than in the small, orderly camp of Auschwitz I. They sought and found each other in the food-transport Kommandos and on many other occasions. Through their work, the Kapos and other foremen in particular had ample opportunity to come into contact with women. A lot of the female Kommandos were even led by male prisoners and many a woman counted herself lucky to have a 'rich' boyfriend – for instance one of the men who worked on the bread wagons and had an abundant supply of bread to satisfy his girlfriend's hunger for food, out of gratitude for her satisfying his hunger for love.

One evening Hans met a prisoner who had been in Buchenwald. They talked about the 'evil' of Auschwitz, where the moral degeneration of the Häftlinge seemed more advanced than in any other camp.

'At Buchenwald the political prisoners have succeeded, after a long struggle, in gaining control over the entire internal leadership of the camp. They even had the cooperation of a few SS people along the way. If a green – a professional criminal – got too big for his boots, he'd get a note telling him to report to the infirmary. One injection and that was him taken care of.'

'Are conditions a lot better there than here?' Hans asked.

'"Organizing" doesn't exist at Buchenwald, only concerted theft from the SS stores for the benefit of all. A cook who steals something from the kitchen gets beaten to death on the spot. Anybody who swaps cigarettes for food is severely punished.'

It wasn't like that at Auschwitz. There, everyone spent the whole day thinking about how to filch as much as possible, and mostly at the expense of their comrades. There were complete black markets in the free minutes after roll call.

'In Buchenwald the political prisoners boycotted the brothel. No Dutchman ever set foot in it,' the Buchenwalder claimed. 'It's not like that here. Anybody who's not Jewish and is therefore allowed in the brothel uses it as much as possible, and the illegal intercourse between men and women here in Birkenau is out-and-out prostitution.'

Hans disagreed. 'You can't apply concepts from normal society to camp conditions. If a girl gives herself for a piece of bread or a litre of soup, you mustn't judge too severely.'

'But it's just the same with prostitutes,' the Buchenwalder said. 'How often doesn't it happen that a woman gets pregnant from a love affair, gives birth to an illegitimate child and is abandoned by the man? She gets excluded from all kinds of circles and prostitution is the only way she has left to provide for herself and the child.'

They had to rush all day long. Hans was in a building-yard Kommando. Long lines of men carrying bricks non-stop. Sometimes it would be railway sleepers or heavy steel girders that scraped the skin off their shoulders. They weren't hit much. The actual punishment detail no longer existed. Now and then they'd catch a blow or a boot, but it was rare for someone to be beaten to death at work.

A year earlier things had been very different. At work Hans had spoken to a Greek who had told him in a surge of self-reproach that he had once given a mate who had been beaten half to death a couple of extra kicks. At that stage, the rule in the camp had been that you weren't allowed to leave the dead lying on the ground at roll call, but had to take them inside. Those kicks meant he was able to carry the body away with a friend and got to spend half a day resting. Another time, the Greek was in a bunk in the hospital next to someone who was severely ill and seemed unconscious. He had taken the man's bread to eat it, but the poor wretch had started yelling. If people had realized the Greek had stolen the sick man's bread, they would have beaten him to within an inch of his life. That was why he pressed his hand over the other man's mouth, but still he wouldn't shut up. He'd pressed and pressed until the man suffocated. Hans asked the Buchenwalder what he, with his superior camp ethics, thought of this. Hans himself considered every method to stay alive in the camp permissible, as long as it wasn't at the expense of a comrade.

A Dutch Catholic, a medical student, joined the conversation: 'My Jesuit once gave me an example: two men are sitting on a wooden raft that can only carry one person. One pushes the other off and he drowns. Does that make him guilty? No, because if one of the two hadn't died, they would have both been lost.'

As an ethical guideline, Hans found that rather opportunistic, but acceptable if necessary. The example wasn't applicable to the Greek though, because he hadn't saved his life with that one piece of bread. If he carried on like that, he would be forced to kill someone else for another piece of bread the next day, and again the day after. If it comes down to 'you or me', everybody says 'me', but it wasn't like that in the camp. You could obtain advantages for yourself at the expense of others, but you couldn't save your life. And since no ethical system – Christian or humanistic – can approve of obtaining an advantage at the expense of greater suffering by others, the Greek's behaviour was indefensible.

Conversations like this were rare, as by the time the work was done and the Kommandos had been dismissed, it was roll call, which sometimes took half an hour but often went on for two hours or more. It didn't matter whether it was mild spring weather or pelting down hail. Then, after roll call, a long queue for bread, often followed by all kinds of inspections: a clothing inspection, for instance, to see whether there might be a button missing from your striped gala costume and to make sure your shoes were clean, i.e. not covered in mud.

If you took each of the factors separately, it was possible to live in one of these Kommandos. The work was heavy, but in itself bearable. The blows hurt, but you weren't beaten to death. You didn't get much bread and soup, but it would have sustained a life of indolence. But the combination of all these elements – so much work and the blows with so little food – was unbearable. And the worst thing was the lack of rest. Work, roll call, inspections, fetching food and, when you were finally lying on a bunk in a motley company of eight men from all over Europe, the futile battle against lice and fleas. Dozing off, waking up, scratching. Then getting yourself under control again. Lie still. Just let the lice crawl. Going back to sleep, waking up again. Arguing with your neighbour. Then you've scratched your leg open, you feel blood, that's going to turn into a sore, please, no more scratching. Then you've done it again! Exhaustion and no rest, feeling deeply miserable.

At night you have to get up – sometimes three times – from the soup and early cardiac weakness. That means climbing over three men and having to walk a few hundred metres to the latrine, a board floor with no less than forty holes in it.

Outside there's a sentry to make sure nobody urinates outdoors. You'd get a thrashing.

Your neighbour, who's some kind of Balkan peasant, is more practical. He's smuggled a food bowl into bed with him and doesn't have to get up. But who's going to eat out of that bowl in the morning? No, you couldn't bring yourself to do that. It's better to walk two hundred metres.

At four in the morning you get up. Vests off, wash. A few drops of water, no soap. Dry yourself with your vest. Often you don't even get a turn at the tap. Maybe you'll find a puddle with rainwater on the way. Then – it's still not dawn – turning out, counting the Kommando. After standing for a long, long time, the Kommando sets off. At the gate the head Kapo reports: 'Building yard, 693 men.' Fear! If it's too many, if 660 are enough, the Obersturmführer will count off 33 at random. They'll be ordered to one side. Nobody will ever see them again.

What you do see is the flame, the eternal flame from the crematorium chimney. Day and night, the fire. Always the awareness that people are burning there. People like yourself, with a brain and a heart that pumps their blood – that miraculous liquid – through an endless network of blood vessels, alive in all their fibres, in their most insignificant cells. God's miraculous creation.

Sometimes the weather is damp and smoke hangs over the camp. That smell of scorched meat, of steak being fried in a pan that hasn't been greased properly. That's your breakfast because you don't have any bread left anyway. At times like that you can't bear it any more. You're tired, sick and disgusted by yourself, because you are a man and the SS, too, are 'men'.

After five weeks the letter: 'I've tracked you down! A man who delivers wood to your camp's kitchen has found you. I'll speak to the Lagerarzt. Stick it out a little longer.'

It took another week before the block clerk came to get him. Hans was checked out at the administrative building and sent back to Auschwitz.

BLOCK 9 HAD UNDERGONE a great change. There was a new Blockältester.

The previous week the Lagerarzt had come to select the Mussulmen. When the lorries arrived a day later to pick up the unlucky men, one was missing, an Italian Jew. Enormous tumult. In the evening the man came back of his own accord. He had turned out with the building-yard Kommando and spent the whole day lugging bags of cement. When the job was finished, the foreman had even praised him for his application. He had only wanted to prove that he wasn't a Mussulman, that he was still able to work hard.

The Lagerarzt, who came back the next day, wasn't receptive to that logic. He had the man taken away immediately and then called in Paul. His letting something like that happen in his block was a scandal. He'd given the Jew a thorough beating at least, he hoped. But Paul was obstinate and, since falling in love with a Jewish girl, had developed a deep empathy for the Jews in the camp.

'I don't beat sick people.'

Then the Lagerarzt began bellowing that in the end Communist riff-raff always showed their true colours. They were Jew-lovers, scum, filthy red swine. The grand physician punched Paul right in the face. Twice, three times, until blood was pouring from his lips. Half an hour later there was a new Blockältester. It was Zlobinsky, a Pole, the former doorkeeper

142

of Block 21. He had a reputation for being sly and coarse. He was difficult, inspected beds, screamed if there was a single straw on the floor, and harried everyone to work as hard as they possibly could.

But after a couple of weeks he fell in love with a girl from Block 10. From then on he spent the whole day sitting at the window and the Pfleger could doze off again and let the room orderlies – recovering patients – do all of the work.

The day after his return, Hans went next door to Block 10 with the kettle Kommando to see Friedel. They were so happy his adventure had turned out well.

'How did you pull it off?' he asked.

'I just went to Klein, the Lagerarzt, explained what had happened, and that you were my husband, and then he wrote down your number.'

'It's incomprehensible. That's the same dog who kicked out Paul last week, after first holding a selection. At the start of the month he was in Birkenau and cleared out the entire Czech family Lager in two days. A thousand men were put on work transport. Five and a half thousand went up the chimney: older men, women and children.'

'You see that often. You can't reason with the younger SS at all, but the older ones, who commit crimes on a grand scale, are sometimes humane in minor things, like now, with you.'

'I don't think that's a point in their favour,' Hans said. 'On the contrary. The youngsters have been raised in the spirit of blood and soil. They don't know any better. But those older ones, like the Lagerarzt, show through those minor acts that they still harbour a remnant of their upbringing. They didn't learn this inhumanity from an early age and had no need to embrace it. That's why they're guiltier than the young Nazi sheep, who have never known better.'

They talked for a while longer. Friedel told him about the injections with malarial blood and the high fevers the women suffered as a result of the artificially induced malaria. It was now easy to get into Block 10 and less dangerous to stay there.

Large groups of Poles were being put on transports regularly and that gave the Jews opportunities to occupy better positions. They could now work in the *Bekleidungskammer* and the photographic studio. There were even a few in the kitchen, and Jewish doctors were no longer limited by preference to the filthiest jobs, but actually did some real medical work. As a result it was now possible for a Jew to go into Block 10 under the pretext of some job or other, whereas previously the Poles had kept such pleasant tasks to themselves.

On the one hand, then, the Polish transports gave them a much more bearable life; on the other, it made them very anxious. The Poles were put on transports, as were the Russians. The Reich Germans, inasmuch as they weren't political prisoners, were incorporated into the SS. All this was clearly influenced by the German withdrawals and the constantly approaching front.

Now – in the summer of 1944 – the Russians had already reached Radom, midway between Lemberg and Krakow. That was only two hundred kilometres from Auschwitz. The next offensive could reach the camp. What would happen to its inmates then?

There were various opinions circulating: an evacuation of the camp, for one. That wouldn't be simple, because although its occupation rate was greatly reduced, the entire Auschwitz complex still held some 120,000 prisoners. Others were convinced the Germans would exterminate them all. There were very few optimists who believed they would let the witnesses to their outrages fall into Russian hands alive.

They were living in a turmoil of growing tension.

In July, a climax: 'The Führer is dead. Wehrmacht and SS are fighting each other everywhere. The generals have taken over the government.' Never before had rumours like these done the rounds and been believed so firmly.

But although it was even claimed the next day that the war was over and a new German government had begun negotiations with the Allies, the SS remained at their posts. Despite this, the rumours were closer to the truth than ever before. Days later they read in an already outdated newspaper – which the non-Jews were allowed to subscribe to – how the Von Witzleben* affair had played out in reality.

The rumours that circulated in the camp were always a caricature, an exaggeration of reality, but you could be sure that there was something going on, even though it was often difficult to discover the true scale of the facts.

It was like that with Block 10 too. For half a year now there had been constant talk of Block 10 being relocated. A new barracks complex had been built a couple of hundred metres from the camp. The SS had moved in, and one building was supposedly for Block 10.

---

* Erwin Von Witzleben, a German officer, was a lead conspirator in the failed plot to assassinate Hitler in 1944. He was tried and sentenced to death on 7 August by the Nazi 'People's Court', known as the *Volksgerichtshof*, which had jurisdiction over so-called political offences.

Always that fear of their approaching separation. But nothing happened. Until in August the rumour took on a more concrete form. Five of the new buildings were going to be women's blocks. Block 10 would be housed there along with the better female Kommandos, like those working in the SS laundry and the munitions factories.

And suddenly, the day of the move arrived. For hours the women stood lined up outside: counting, counting and counting again. Nobody understood what they were waiting for, but Hans and Friedel were glad of it. There were hardly any SS around and they could talk at length, longer than ever. This farewell turned into their longest and calmest conversation for a year. Hans wanted to know what would happen to them in the new block.

'I think they'll just continue the experiments. This week they were working under high pressure in Block 10. Apparently nobody was allowed to go to the new block who's not on the Clauberg and Goebel list and that means being injected at least once. The staff weren't exempt any more either.'

'And you – how did you manage to get out of it?' Hans asked, terrified that she was about to admit what he had feared for so long. Never had they given up hope of coming through it all alive and if Friedel had been '*gespritzt*' she might be permanently infertile. She could tell how scared he was.

'There were thirty-four nurses and other staff who hadn't been through it yet. We all had to come before Clauberg to explain why we hadn't had our turn yet and to hear when we had to come in for the test. Those who refused would be sent to Birkenau. When I was standing before him, I told him I was suffering from an inflammation of the renal pelvis. "Yes," he said, "it's not possible at the moment then. That could be fatal." Fortunately nobody checked me because I got over that inflammation a month ago.'

It was astonishing that she had said the one thing that hit the mark. She was a layman, but must have had wondrous intuition.

Towards midday the women marched off. Now they would no longer be able to see each other whenever they wanted to, but the men who worked in the new blocks could still deliver letters and packages. Friedel would try to come into the camp to see the dentist or the radiologist as often as she could, and that would allow them to still meet.

Most of the men knew nothing about their wives at all. Some, like Eli, knew that they were dead, but even those who knew their wives were in an adjoining camp, like Birkenau for instance, had never had any opportunity to contact them. Hans and Friedel still had nothing to complain about.

Roll call was over and Hans and Eli were walking along Birkenallee. It was still oppressively hot. Later it would be crowded here, but most of the Häftlinge were still in their blocks waiting for their bread. For the moment there were only some prominents and Pfleger around. Sitting on a bench were Dr Valentin and Professor Mansfeld. Valentin called out to Hans, 'So, are you back to normal again now?'

Hans hadn't realized he'd been acting abnormally. They sat down on the grass next to their older colleagues. 'Being sad seems very normal to me,' Hans said.

'That face of yours the whole day long. What have you got to complain about? You'll be sure to find another opportunity to get in touch with your wife.'

'Yes, but nowhere near as easily, and if she gets into difficulties of any kind I won't be able to help her.'

'What kind of difficulties could come up now?' the professor asked.

'You'd be surprised, Prof,' Eli replied. 'There's still a lot they're capable of. First of all, there are two X-ray rooms in that new block. They can work on an even larger scale than in Block 10. Or you might have heard of those new test experiments they're going to do. There's a row of small rooms in the new block that are apparently intended for bringing women together with men. Then you can see from the result whether or not the sterilization method was effective.'

Hans didn't believe it. 'Come on now, there are so many stories. There's also constant talk of a Jewish brothel that's going to be opened on the first of September.'

Eli thought the two rumours had to be based on something. 'Maybe the tests will be carried out in a kind of brothel.'

'Then I hope there's not a single man who makes use of it.'

Professor Mansfeld joined the conversation. 'Don't be ridiculous. If they take it into their heads to try something like that, you won't have any opportunity to dissuade them.'

'His wife hasn't even been injected. What is there to test?' Eli said.

'Ah, that doesn't mean much one way or the other,' the professor continued. 'You can't expect any logic from our overlords. Their experiments are neither logical nor systematic. They're just whims. Whatever pops into their head, they try it out. Last month in a camp near Köningshütte, an Oberscharführer locked three men and three women up with each other in a small room for several days. He took away all their clothes and observed their behaviour closely. Then he stuffed one of the men with food, let another eat normally and didn't give the third anything at all. He was trying to test the influence of nutrition on sexual performance. Even a child understands that something like that is too insane.'

Hans agreed. 'Exactly, that's just a personal whim. Take those tests with sedatives for instance. Last week an SS man came into Block 19 and picked out three men. They were given a powder, dissolved in real coffee. Shortly afterwards they fell asleep. Two never woke up again, the third happened to come to after thirty-six hours. I can imagine how they hit on "research" like that. The gentleman from the SS was a little upset by the Von Witzleben affair and couldn't get to sleep at night. In his home apothecary he found some powders from Canada, but he was a bit timid about trying them. So why not a "scientific experiment" with a few Häftlinge?'

Eli interrupted him. 'It's nonsense to even try to analyse an experiment like that. A waste of time. That experiment at Königshütte is nothing more than the perverse gratification of a man who wanted to observe those people's sex lives. Experiments like the ones in Block 10 are a different matter.'

'Wrong, Sir,' the professor snapped. 'From a humanitarian and scientific perspective, none of the experiments carried out by Germans, in fact all of German science since 1933, has been a hair better. A major factor, of course, has been the expulsion of all Jewish scholars. Throughout the history of German science there have been remarkably large numbers of Jewish and foreign scholars. You find an especially large number of Poles among "German" scientists. People like Copernicus have been annexed in the propaganda to demonstrate German superiority!'

'What if Hitler hadn't kicked out the Jews?'

'German science still wouldn't have produced much. After all, science means: investigate and conclude. In Germany the conclusion is determined in advance. It has to agree with state dogma. As long as it's about purely technical discoveries – for the war industry or in the field of medicine – research results are happily accepted, but as soon as a German scholar ventures into historical or philosophical territory, he knows in advance which conclusion his research has to lead to, and if he's stupid enough to come up with a result that conflicts with National Socialist doctrine, he won't last long.'

'I understand all of that perfectly, Professor. But getting back to our women. These are purely technical experiments here, so they can be carried out properly.'

'Science is a system that has developed in service of human society. For that reason alone, research into mass sterilization can't be set up scientifically. Because German science doesn't serve humanity, but the German race. In any case, look at the practice. Who is playing a role here? Clauberg, Goebel, people from the Gestapo, and Samuel, who's trying to save his own skin. The experiments are carried out by a *Scharführer* who doesn't have a clue and derives his authority from a former career as a toothbrush salesman. No, Sir, research that goes against every human principle has nothing to do with science. If one of my former lab assistants had treated a laboratory animal the way the women are treated here, I would have marched him to the door myself.'

Mansfeld's account made a great impression on them, but no sooner had he finished than the Block 9 messenger came up to them: they had to go straight back. They were moving to Block 8 that same evening. For a couple of hours they had to work hard: dismantling cabinets and tables, and packing medicaments. But fortunately a countermand arrived: moving tomorrow.

It was an arduous day's work: carrying patients, straw mattresses and beds. Block 8 was a filthy, run-down quarantine block. Blocks 9 and 10 were going to be used for Gypsies. Entire families: men, women and masses of children. They were privileged prisoners who, for unknown reasons, had escaped Birkenau and were being sent to camps in Germany. Generally it was no different for the Gypsies than for the Jews. They were a much smaller group than the Jews and had occupied a much less important social position in the various European countries, but in Birkenau they went 'up the chimney' all the same. Yet more proof that the persecution of the Jews was not essentially an 'anti-capitalist struggle against the global Jewish plutocracy'.

Practised in hate, the SS was an organ for the oppression of their own German people and related nations. They rehearsed their methods on the Jews, Russians and Gypsies under the motto of racial purification. The camps of Ellecom, in the Netherlands on the edge of the Veluwe, and Stutthof, near Danzig,* were officially considered SS training camps – *Schulungslager*. In the camps, the members of the SS were able to satisfy the sadistic tendencies that had been aroused in them, and because they were given these opportunities of satisfaction, they remained obedient followers of Hitler until the end.

After a week, they had cleaned the block and done it up a little. The patients were covered with blankets that were still soiled from their predecessors. They were wearing vests that were 'disinfected once a month' but never washed and therefore marked with brown bloodstains and spotted black with

---

* Gdansk (Danzig in German), on the Baltic coast of Poland.

flea dirt. But at first sight everything was clean, the floors were shining white and the beds nicely painted. It had been an expensive week because they didn't get any official supplies and had to pay for the paint for the beds and doors with food, bread and margarine that was, therefore, no longer available for the patients.

Unfortunately more Gypsies arrived on the ninth day and Block 8 moved to Block 7. There were now two thousand Gypsies in the camp and it was a bigger mess than ever. After all, Auschwitz was a 'bad' camp. A barbed-wire fence was erected around the three Gypsy blocks and there were always two sentries on duty, but that didn't prevent a brisk trade from developing at the wire.

The Gypsies received more bread than the others and used it to buy sausage and potatoes, which were smuggled into the camp by the ordinary prisoners. This led to a devaluation of bread. Whereas a ration of bread was initially worth twelve potatoes, you could now only get seven for it.

The Gypsies played music and danced all day, and the men at the fence feasted their eyes until the guards chased them off with blows or subjected them to punishments for loitering around the camp during work time. But things got even more out of hand after dark. Then men from the camp would find a way into the Gypsy blocks and a lot of the Gypsy women would slip through the barbed-wire fencing to fill their own stomachs properly for once and sweeten the lives of the Blockälteste and Kapos, who often had a room of their own in the work blocks. Although they could also get by without a room, as long as there was something to eat and drink.

Raids in the middle of the night. The SS searching for women in all the beds in the whole camp. So many victims!

Every morning the barbed wire needed to be repaired again. Hans didn't like the uproar. Seeing the Gypsies enjoying themselves only made you more intensely aware of everything you were missing in the camp. It made you feel even more like someone who has been buried alive. He had little interest in the Gypsy women.

The time he used to spend outside Friedel's window, talking to her, he now spent upstairs with fellow doctors or talking to Professor Frijda, the Amsterdam professor of economics, who had been a patient in the Krankenbau for a week now. The old man had arrived on the last Dutch transport. By chance he'd got in the right line after getting off the train. In Auschwitz he was put in the roadworks Kommando. After just a few weeks of dragging wagons all day, he hadn't been able to hold up any longer and had been admitted to hospital. He was soon very popular among the doctors because of his friendly, modest attitude. They found '*le professeur hollandais*' '*très charmant*'. But for Hans he was a great worry.

In the mornings, even before the gong, the men were already jostling at the windows of Block 7, which was opposite Block 8, to see the women washing themselves. Then the Blockältester came and chased the patients back into bed. But he didn't come into the *Pflegerstube* and the Pfleger amused themselves at length with erotic sign-language conversations with Gypsy women in various states of undress.

In a situation where even Saint Anthony would have succumbed to temptation, Hans did look across at the other block now and then, but only fleetingly, because seeing women only heightened his longing for Friedel.

Maintaining communication hadn't been easy. Krebs, the Dutch dental technician, had already spent a few days in the bunker for passing on letters to the women. A letter from Hans had been among them. During his interrogation, Krebs had explained that it was a letter from a man to his own wife. There was nothing special in it. Krebs was one of the few Dutch prominents and that was lucky for him, because with the help of his boss, the Obersturmführer of the dental clinic, the matter was soon settled.

Friedel's hospital visit hadn't gone well either. She did come each Wednesday when the girls came to the Krankenbau for their consultations, but the SDG was always there. He was a dirty character, a Romanian. The foreign SS men were always even crueller than the Germans. He gave the girls a hard time, stood over them while they were being examined and then often disappeared upstairs with one of them, taking her to one of the opticians' or chemists' rooms.

The lads would quickly seize the opportunity to talk to their wives. This time it was Hans, Majzel and De Hond, who had been let in for a moment by the second SDG. Friedel told him about the new block. There weren't any experiments there. The girls had been allocated to all kinds of Kommandos. She was on a night shift, making clothes. It wasn't easy: twelve hours on the go in an attic, in the dust, sewing old rags, and if she didn't complete her quota they hit her. She couldn't bear the dust and couldn't stop coughing. It wasn't long before the Romanian was back again. He'd been drinking and made some filthy remarks before chasing out all of the men.

When would he see Friedel again? He had to think of something better. That was on Wednesday. On Thursday all the Gypsies left, and on Friday they had to move again. They were going back to Block 9, which was now very much the worse for wear.

The next morning: 'Achtung, Lagerarzt!' He didn't go to the wards, where it was still a great mess, but headed straight to the Blockältester's room, where he spoke to the head doctor for a few minutes. After he was gone, Zielina called all of the doctors into outpatients.

A list had to be made of all patients. Next to the names the doctor had to fill in whether or not the patient could be discharged, and if not, how much longer he would have to stay in the hospital: one, two, three weeks, or longer than three. Their expressions were dark because they realized that there was something nasty behind it, and the discussion grew heated as they tried to identify the limit: how long someone would be allowed to be sick without risking the gas chamber.

Hans spent a long time talking to Flechner, the French doctor who was treating Frijda, about the professor's fate. They couldn't say he was healthy. If they did, he would be discharged immediately and at the moment he couldn't walk a hundred metres. But they didn't dare say 'longer than three weeks' either. That would seal his fate. To make matters worse, the Lagerarzt had taken all of the index cards with him, so simply making the professor disappear by hiding him was no longer an option.

They called in Zielina and decided together to write down three weeks. There is no decision in his life that Hans regrets as much.

The next day the card index was returned – except the cards of the Jews who had to stay in the hospital for more than two weeks. These patients were to be picked up the next day 'to be put to work at the Birkenau Weaving Mill in a light Kommando'. The Birkenau Weaving Mill was 'the world's biggest factory'. Under this pretext they had already taken a couple of million people to the gas chamber.

Zielina gave Hans Sunday morning off. The Kapo of the roadworks Kommando was a friend of Leen Sanders's and – thanks to Leen's recommendation and a packet of cigarettes contributed for this purpose by a Polish patient – willing to let Hans turn out with his detail. Thirty men were working in the new female camp and they smuggled Hans in with them.

He wasn't the only guest. At least half of the Sunday Kommando was interested in the girls. The SS hadn't latched on to this trick yet and as a result they could walk around the female camp relatively undisturbed. As long as they always had a shovel or a few slabs with them to immediately set to work if an SS man or one of the female overseers was in the vicinity, the Kapo said.

Various lads disappeared into one of the attics with their girlfriends. But Friedel wasn't interested in that kind of 'stolen love'. They stood behind a door in her block and were able to talk undisturbed for a long time. Hans poured out his heart to her about Frijda.

'There's nothing you can do,' Friedel comforted him. 'In most cases where you don't give a patient the best medicine, nobody can blame you for it, although that's much more to be expected from you than making the right choice with a vicious trick like this.'

That was true and Hans tried not to dwell on his feelings of self-reproach.

The next day the lorries came. Hans felt miserable. Off went Professor Frijda, the former rector of the University of Amsterdam, a man who had once presented Queen Wilhelmina with an honorary degree. He shook hands with

Hans and asked him to pass on his regards to his loved ones, should he survive.

'But Professor, you will see them again yourself.'

What else was he supposed to say? He didn't have the courage to simply speak the truth. He had to go along with the lies about Birkenau.

Then an SS man came up and hurried the professor on to the lorry. Dressed in a grimy vest and wearing wooden sandals, one of Holland's best-known and most highly regarded academics climbed up on to the back of the lorry that would take him to the gas chamber.

With the SS you never knew where you were. You witnessed the grossest contradictions: in the morning when thousands marched out five abreast in straight lines to face a day of blows, hunger and murderously hard labour, the orchestra, made up of fifty prisoners, would be playing at the gate. Once the doctors had to compile lists of those who were eligible for supplementary nutrition. The day after the lists were handed in, all of the malnourished misfortunates were hauled off to the gas chamber.

Jewish women – slave labourers – could be thrashed at will. But if an SS man felt the urge, he would just as likely take a Jewish girl: 'And if you're not willing, I'll use force.' If a prisoner was caught 'organizing' a piece of bread, he would be caned. But the trade in gold and diamonds, and in the slaughterhouse (once fourteen pigs in one go), went through the SS.

In the autumn of 1943 a sabotage plot was discovered in Majdanek, the concentration camp near Lublin. The SS then decided to eliminate all eighteen thousand Jews in one day. An enormous right-angled trench was dug. The people undressed in one side of the right angle, then walked around the corner to be gunned down. The racket of the machine guns and the cries of the victims were drowned out by five orchestras.

Lagerarzt Klein was an expert at selections. One evening the entire camp population had to file naked past the Rapportführer in the old laundry. They got undressed outside on Birkenallee. Standing at the entrance were a few Blockälteste, who gave everyone a shove. Those who stumbled over the doorstep were Mussulmen. Those who marched past the gentlemen with their chests puffed up were through. They picked out about a thousand that way and then stuffed them in an empty block. In the night all the non-Jews were released. The next day the Jews filed past the Lagerarzt between Blocks 8 and 9 while he checked whether there weren't perhaps some strong ones left amongst them. He was having an animated conversation with Hössler, the Lagerführer, and mostly had his back to the passing column. Now and then he turned around and picked out someone at random, who was then saved for a while.

IN THE CAMP AT that time, two blocks, 22 and 23, were surrounded by barbed wire. Women were apparently going to be moved into them. In Block 23 they set up a small outpatients clinic.

Friedel began looking worse and worse. She couldn't cope with the night shifts in the sewing workshop and was coughing more and more, and regularly running a temperature. Hans decided to go to the Lagerarzt to ask if she could be sent to the new outpatients as a *Pflegerin*.

Valentin, the head doctor of the upstairs wards, thought Hans had gone mad. The Lagerarzt would just 'smash him in the gob'. He could kick him out of the hospital into a heavy Kommando for that kind of impudence. You weren't even allowed to know your wife was here, let alone speak to the Lagerarzt about it.

But Hans was counting on the inconsistency, the split personality these SS officers displayed. And sure enough, the same man who had dispatched thousands to their deaths because they were sick or weak was happy for Friedel to be transferred from the sewing workshop to the outpatients in Block 23 'because the dust in those old clothes was giving her such a terrible cough'.

After the mass selection that claimed Professor Frijda, the Krankenbau was half empty. The Pfleger started to worry. 'If there's another selection like that, they'll get rid of a bunch of Pfleger at the same time. There's far too many.'

With danger approaching, there was a sudden need to be heroic. Whereas before nobody had thought of resistance, they now felt that they couldn't simply surrender. One evening Klempfner, a Czech doctor from the upstairs ward, summoned Hans and Eli Polak to his room.

'There's an organization in the camp. Naturally, I can't tell you any details, but in our block there are now fifteen people willing to follow me. Will you join us?'

'Of course,' Eli said. 'What have we got to lose?'

'If something's about to happen, I'll send for one of you to come and receive instructions. Then it will all be clear.'

It never got that far. After about a week the order came: Block 9 was being dissolved. The patients and Pfleger were moving to Block 19 (another hospital block, which was also half empty). Hans's ward would remain intact. Zielina was being kept on as head doctor. In Block 19 the Blockältester was Sepp Rittner: a gigantic fellow, a Communist who'd already spent eight years in camps, but always with sunny Viennese humour, '*Wiener Blut*', that refused to be cooled by Prussian tyranny. Hans had known him since coming to Auschwitz and they were close friends. Now the good life could begin.

In Block 19 Hans rose and became a prominent. Ochodsky, the ward doctor, had been put on a transport, and Zielina, who had now taken on the treatment of the non-Jewish patients, left more or less everything to Hans.

Now that he was treating patients, he didn't need to do the dirty work any more, and as he was in much closer contact with them, he was also given much more from their packages.

He went to visit Friedel every day to take her some of his treasures. After all, she was now back in a block in the same camp. Of course, it was dangerous! In just the first weeks, two men were shot dead while trying to talk to the women at the fence. On Sunday evening it was an eighteen-year-old boy. He had discovered his sister, who he hadn't seen for half a year. But the greatest frauds always stay unpunished the longest. That was what Hans was counting on as he strolled through the gate to Block 23 every day holding a sphygmomanometer or a bottle under one arm. Sometimes he was carrying scales with a fellow doctor. The more they caught the eye, the better. And if an SS guard asked any questions, they were doctors at work, on their way to the female outpatients.

The only danger was the SDG, a Romanian Rottenführer, who knew all too well that Hans had absolutely no business being there. On one occasion he did catch them, when Hans and Friedel were sitting down together to talk. He threatened them and kicked Hans out, but didn't take it any further.

On a Sunday soon after New Year, Alfonso Colet came up to Hans. Colet was the new Kapo in disinfection. He was a Spaniard, one of the many Loyalists who had fled Franco. In France he had fallen into German hands – out of the fat and into the fire – and ended up in a concentration camp. Here in Auschwitz he was the central figure in a small group of Spaniards and *Rotspanier*, 'Spanish Reds', who were Germans who had fought on the side of the government in the Spanish Civil War and been handed over to Hitler by Franco, then sent to concentration camps.

'You coming to Block 23?' Colet asked.

'What's your excuse?'

'Nobody questions me. Anyway, tomorrow my lads are disinfecting Block 23. That's why I want to go there today to have a look at what needs to be done.'

Colet was friends with Sara, the acting Blockälteste, a Belgian. He and Hans set off after the midday soup and spent the whole afternoon at Block 23 in the Blockältestes' room, talking nineteen to the dozen with the women and having a great time. Later they were joined by a Kapo from the kitchen block who was having a relationship with the Blockälteste and arrived with a bottle of gin.

The block clerk was at the fence as a lookout and would raise the alarm if an SS man was heading for the women's blocks. The men from the work details who wanted to look at the girls on their free Sunday afternoon had been driven off with blows, but it never occurred to the guards that anybody could be as brazen as Colet and Hans. Stealing half a million is safer than stealing half a guilder.

Colet told them about the new Jewish Lagerältester. Since all of the Poles had been put on transports and most of the Germans had been conscripted into the SS, almost everyone left in the camp was Jewish. As a result they had even appointed a Jewish Lagerältester, but after two days the man had gone mad; he had developed megalomania. He was lying on his bed in his room when Kaduk, the second Rapportführer, came in and ordered him to get up. But the Lagerältester said that he wouldn't dream of letting Kaduk order him around and that he, as Lagerältester, was not the Rapportführer's errand boy. They had an enormous row and the Lagerältester was now in the bunker.

The women laughed heartily because for someone in a concentration camp it really is very funny to hear about a

Häftling, even the Lagerältester, behaving like that to the Rapportführer.

Hans was better informed: 'What happened isn't funny at all. Alfonso's story is the official version, the one the SS is putting about. In reality the case is very different. Red Cross packages came for the camp and the Germans needed a signature from a prisoners' representative as proof the packages had been distributed. The Lagerältester refused. Now he's in the bunker and he definitely won't be getting out alive.'

The kitchen Kapo's gin proved stronger than the Lagerältester's sad fate, so their spirits weren't dampened too much. They only had three chairs for the six of them, but kept their behaviour within the limits of decency – although the limits of decency were, of course, somewhat different here than they had been at home.

Friedel was too in love to talk very much, but Sara dominated the conversation. She chattered away about the big group of men who had been in the block on New Year's Eve. They had bribed the Blockführer who was on duty with a bottle of gin. Hans had his own information about the resulting party too. Not only had the Jews been able to get on to better work details recently, they were even in the orchestra. Jewish musicians had been brought into Auschwitz from all the nearby camps. They had formed a swing band amongst themselves. All Dutch, because the orchestra's best musicians were Dutch, and definitely when it came to jazz. There was Jack de Vries and Maurice van Kleef, Lex van Weeren and Sally van der Kloot. Also Ab Frank, bandmaster of the Bouwmeester Revue. Hans had played clarinet with them. He'd been there that New Year's Eve too, but had gone straight to Friedel's room. Sara couldn't have known that, and there was no reason she should either.

Half drunk, Sara rattled away. Now about the Sauna. The Sauna was the large washroom with two hundred showers. The Kommando that worked there was the most popular of all. You could see more naked women there than anywhere in the world. Sometimes a thousand at once. The men who worked there could be real swine. Some of them walked among the women and harassed them shamelessly. For a half a packet of margarine you could turn out with the Kommando for a day. If women from Birkenau were coming to wash that day, tough luck, because that was a nasty sight. All those worn-out, emaciated bodies, almost as dirty after washing as before. But if the women were from Auschwitz, from the better Kommandos, then ...

The most brazen were the SS, of course, who went there for their entertainment. They made the women do gymnastics for them and carried out 'inspections'. A girl here in the block was already pregnant.

Friedel and Hans were not as animated as the others. It was all great fun, an afternoon like that, but being so close to each other made the longing grow so much – the longing for freedom, for a home, for children, for life. They were privileged, unique among the thousands here, but even the benefits were a poor substitute.

Hans grew sombre. He always got like that when he drank. Friedel tried to cheer him up, stroking his head and joking about his going bald. But he spoke of the future and the decision that was almost upon them. Yesterday's newspaper had reported for the first time on the Russian offensive. The Russians had mounted an attack and the Germans needed to 'shorten the front to gain time for the necessary countermeasures to take effect'. The decision couldn't be far away now. The front was only 150 kilometres from Auschwitz. The tension was rising.

The tension kept rising. On Tuesday evening the newspapers wrote about '*Distrikt Krakau*'. On Wednesday the *Krakauer Zeitung* didn't arrive. There were more and more air-raid alarms, more and more blackouts, undoubtedly caused by partisans. Sometimes in the night they could already hear the artillery – if dull and very distant. Wednesday evening: Hans and Eli were working in the outpatients in Block 28. They were on duty there once a week. It was awful work. You only had a few pieces of paper and a bit of ointment to dress wounds. To get an aspirin for a patient you had to work through a mountain of bureaucracy and then mostly there turned out to be nothing available anyway. Unless the patient had cigarettes or margarine – then he could sort it out with the outpatients Pfleger, who did have dressings and aspirin. He in turn bought them from the prisoners who worked in the SS infirmary, where the attics were full of inexhaustible supplies: bandages, medicaments, toiletries, whatever you wanted. The prisoners got almost none of that through official channels. But Hans had something in his pocket: a roll of sticking plaster and some gauze. He either 'organized' it at the Block 19 outpatients or bought it himself to dress the Dutch patients' wounds. He had bread to spare and couldn't take it all to Friedel.

As a result they were soon surrounded by Dutch patients. It was slow working by candlelight; chaos had crept in. All over outpatients, small groups were engaged in intense discussion. The issue that was preoccupying them: evacuation, extermination or surrendering to the Russians? None of them came to a conclusion. Everything was equally plausible.

Later in the evening some women came with a female patient who needed an operation. Dr Alina Brewda was with them. For a half a year she had been the Blockälteste of Block 10 – until she refused to cooperate with a particular experiment. She was Friedel's guardian angel and, as such, Hans knew her well.

A female overseer and a Blockführer had accompanied the women, but they couldn't escape the tension either and left them to their fate. Brewda came over to Hans and asked him what the men thought of it all.

He didn't know, he was just glad the end was in sight.

Brewda was in a dark mood. She had seen too much. She was from Warsaw, where half a million Jews had been squeezed into the ghetto, which had room for 150,000. From there they were successively carted off. Once in Treblinka, the SS killed 23,000 in a single day, probably their record. More even than the 18,000 in one day in Majdanek. The Warsaw Jews saw that there was no way out and the uprising began. That was in April 1943.

They got weapons from the Poles outside the ghetto and hid in the old buildings. The SS had great difficulty forcing their way through the streets and when they finally had the ghetto in their hands, armed Jews were still concealed everywhere in the cellars and the sewage canals that are so numerous in an old city. The entrances to the cellars were camouflaged: you slid a sink cabinet to one side or raised a rug. At night they emerged and carried out bloodbaths among the SS occupiers. Unable to gain control over these underground forces, they were left with only one option: they mined all of the houses and blew them up.

'Only a few thousand escaped,' said Brewda, 'like me.'

Later they all fell into the hands of the SS again. The uprising in the Warsaw Ghetto was a case study of a people's war. It was doomed to failure. Half a million badly armed Jews couldn't win the war against Hitler. There are still hundreds of thousands buried under the rubble, but they dragged more than 20,000 SS troops into the grave with them.

WHEN A CHILD STARTS to cry, the mother wakes from the deepest sleep. Even if the sensory contact with the outside world has been broken in sleep, the mind remains alert, especially if we're expecting something. At three in the morning the gong began to sound and within a few seconds the whole camp was in an uproar. Hans dressed quickly. When he got outside he saw men streaming out of all of the blocks and lining up as if for roll call. Evacuation, after all. It was bitterly cold and fine snow was drifting down. But nobody seemed to feel it. Everyone was too excited because the end was approaching. Whatever happened, Auschwitz was finished.

Blocks 23 and 24 were still completely dark.

Hans went back into the Krankenbau to ask Sepp what they had to do.

'Nothing,' Sepp said. 'There aren't any instructions yet for the sick. And anyway, we don't have any clothes for them. I'm not letting them go like this.'

Sepp was right and Hans urged people to stay calm. But almost everyone had got out of bed and many of them were walking around the camp, looking for friends they wanted to say goodbye to.

Half an hour after the gong, there was a roll call. The numbers weren't right anywhere. But what could they do? The roll call was abandoned and the men had to form up in their Kommandos, like every other morning.

At five the first groups left. They were made up of non-vital Kommandos like roadworks and river gravel. The factory and food-production Kommandos were going to stay.

Even as they were marching off, rumours arose that, as always, were a clear reflection of people's hopes. 'Half are going on transport now. The rest will stay and carry on working. The machines will all be carted off and we'll stay until the Russians get here.'

Long lines of farmers' wagons were driven into the camp. They loaded up bread and preserves from the kitchen storerooms and then set off after the transports that had left. Meanwhile the lights had gone on in Block 23. Hans went around to the back. Nobody was watching out to see if anybody was standing by the barbed wire. But how to catch their attention? He whistled all kinds of tunes. Then he tried the Belgian national anthem, *La Brabançonne.* That worked. Sara opened her window. Yes, she would call Friedel.

'Friedel, stay as long as you can!'

'Sweetheart, no, that's much too dangerous.'

'Listen to me.'

They disagreed. Then Friedel had to go. She needed to arrange clothes. Later, when it was light, Hans would try to get into the block.

He walked back past the long lines of those who were leaving. They were shivering from the cold as they had already been standing outside for a couple of hours and had almost no clothes on. Those few linen rags offered no protection. Some of them had wrapped themselves in blankets. But many hadn't dared. As if keeping the camp intact made any difference now it was being abandoned.

The Pfleger were lined up in Block 19. Sepp had received his instructions. Clothes for the patients were going to be issued in the Bekleidungskammer and they had to go there with stretchers to pick them up.

At eight o'clock the designated Kommandos left. It was now light and Hans was heading back to Block 23 when he bumped into the Rottenführer, who was looking for Pfleger for a job in the women's block. His only option was to lay his cards on the table, asking if he could go with them to say goodbye to his wife. The Romanian grinned.

Friedel was overjoyed to see him. A transport of women had already left and they had searched for her everywhere, but she had hidden in the attic because she still wanted to say goodbye to him. He had only been there a moment when the Rottenführer had someone call him. The Dutchman had to come immediately. There was a coke oven in the attic that needed to be taken to the laundry.

Hans swore, but didn't dare object, and got the oven from the attic. It was an enormous weight, but when Hans was angry that was something he liked. He carried the oven to the laundry in one go and threw it down on the floor. He was standing there catching his breath for a moment when he saw the Rottenführer arriving with the other lads, who weren't carrying anything at all. He'd only made Hans carry it so he couldn't stay there with his wife. That Rottenführer was the bane of his life. But now he'd outsmart him. The Rottenführer went into the Schreibstube with the lads to get all of the paperwork, which had to be burnt.

In the meantime Hans disappeared. Back with Friedel, he was at a loss for words.

'Do you really not want to try to stay?'

'No, they'll finish off everyone who's sick.'

'But that journey will be terrible. Are we up to that?'

'We don't have any choice, Hans. Promise me you'll go too.'

He hesitated. Then he promised, but at the same time he felt that he was being dishonest with her for the first time, because he was scared to death of that journey. In the same instant the door opened. It was Colet.

'I told Sara she had to stay, but she's too scared.'

Hans said he didn't understand the women, but there wasn't anything they could do about it. Then yelling sounded through the block: 'All line up!' The farewell was brief. Friedel was scared of looking weak. As always she couldn't face the feelings that assailed her.

Hans turned at the door, but she raised her hands as if begging him to leave and not make it even more difficult.

The rest of the day was uneventful and Hans felt numbed. For two years they had fought together. They'd had many close calls, but they had never let themselves be parted for long. First at the train – the selection. Then the frightening month he'd spent in Birkenau and, later, after Block 10 had been moved. They had always found each other again. But now?

The next morning the Kapo from the kitchen block came with a letter from Friedel.

Hans, I've been in the women's camp since yesterday. I think you were right. It would be better to stay. That's what everyone here wants, but it won't be possible. If only Sara hadn't been so stupid! They just cleared the block next to ours, beating the girls out with their rifle butts. Anyway, I'll do my best, darling. Be brave. One day we'll see each other again. They're already on their way.

Bye, sweetheart.

He read and reread it. What did she mean, 'If only Sara hadn't been so stupid'? He went to see Colet.

'Yesterday I took three sets of men's clothing to Block 23. For Friedel and the two Saras. But my Sara was too scared.'

Hans could have kicked himself. That would have been the solution: dress them in men's clothing, then do or die together.

'What are you going to do now, Alfonso?'

'We're not leaving, not under any circumstances. You'll see that the rest of the camp will leave today, except maybe the sick. But we're going to hide. We don't want to die in the snow on the side of the road.'

'Where are you going to hide?' Hans asked.

'If you keep your mouth shut, I'll show you.'

Under the enormous pile of dirty clothes in the disinfection cellar, they'd made a concealed hiding place. The cellar was concrete and the building above it was made of wood, so even if it collapsed, they'd still be safe. Alfonso turned out to be well informed.

Around eleven o'clock the Lagerältester ran through the camp like a madman: 'All turn out!' Even the kitchen staff left. The Krankenbau was the only place nothing happened. There were virtually no SS left. They had gone on the marches with the transports and their departure signalled the start of the plundering of the camp.

They fetched clothes from the Bekleidungskammer and tore open the bags in the Effektenkammer, with everyone picking out the best things they could find. The storerooms under the kitchen had been broken open and the patients, who had hardly been able to drag themselves that far, were now sitting down to stuff themselves from tins of meat and barrels of sauerkraut. And what was worse: they'd found vodka in a cellar. Polish vodka that was almost pure alcohol: burning your throat and without the slightest taste.

Late in the afternoon, the first victims: ill, critically ill, vomiting and diarrhoea, deeply miserable, with others rolling over the street or lying stupefied in the gutter, so terribly drunk. The start of an eventful evening.

At eight o'clock the Rottenführer appeared with a few henchmen. Everybody who could walk had to get ready. Almost all of them wanted to go. Only the Poles were willing to stay. They all said they were too sick for a transport, evidently pinning their hopes on the partisans. There were endless discussions about who was in the best condition.

A couple of doctors had to stay in each block. In Block 19 it was Akkerman, a non-Jewish Dutchman, and Hans, who preferred the dangers of the camp to those of the transport. Hans was counting on Colet with his Spaniards.

At ten the Rottenführer bellowed that everyone had to come outside. Then came Sepp's miraculous deed. He locked the door on the inside, took up position in front of it with his feet planted firmly and snarled at anyone who tried to get out: 'You idiot, with your sick body out in the cold, where do you think you'll end up? If the Romanian comes to get you, it will be soon enough.'

But the Romanian didn't come to get them. He only had a few men with him and wasn't equal to the situation. Fully armed, wearing a helmet, with a rifle on his back and a torch in his hand, he still felt unsure of himself now that his cushy life was over too. He didn't even notice that nobody from Block 19 had turned out. Sepp's moment of boldness had saved hundreds of lives.

Once the Krankenbau had marched off, it was very empty in the camp. There were only a few hundred bedridden patients who hadn't been able to leave the three hospital blocks, plus the overcrowded Block 19, full of patients and a wide range of other camp inmates who had gone to Sepp's block to lay low.

Late that night, maybe around eleven, there was an incident. Akkerman had gone out to the kitchen block with a few men to get some food. An SS man was standing in the front square. He must have thought they were looters and opened fire without warning. Akkerman was shot in the stomach. An hour later he was dead. When Hans heard what had happened, he realized the camp could burst into turmoil at any moment. The time to act had come. He went to disinfection.

The Spaniards were in the middle of a heated discussion. Some of them were in favour of hiding in the cellar; others, Colet among them, preferred to flee. They had found a submachine gun in one of the warehouses and if they encountered small groups of SS along the way they would defend themselves.

They decided that Hans and Colet would scout out the situation. In Block 15, which had a view of the gate, the lights were on. It was the fire Kommando, who had been ordered to stay behind. They had dragged a piano out of the concert hall and it was sheer pandemonium. It was like a little boy who is afraid of the dark and hides his fear by singing at the top of his voice. They admitted that their situation was precarious, but didn't have any new information. The Russians hadn't even entered Krakow yet; anything could happen before they reached Auschwitz.

When Hans and Alfonso went outside they heard voices near the gate. It was German – some incomprehensible dialect. They crept past the kitchen block and then, looking around the corner with a small mirror, saw that it was two Wehrmacht soldiers, old men on sentry duty. They slipped back to Block 15, then simply walked down the road to the gate.

'Good evening,' said the soldiers.

'Good evening, are you on sentry duty?'

'Yes, our company's stationed in a building close by.' One of the soldiers wanted to buy Alfonso's watch for some bacon. Alfonso began haggling with him in the hope of finding out more, but a car suddenly drove up. They tried to leave but it was too late. The man in the car called them back. It was *Sturmbannführer* Krause, the one who had just shot Akkerman.

'What are you doing here?'

'We're Pfleger,' Hans said, making up a story. 'We're doing a round. Every hour we have to do a circuit to make sure there's nothing out of the ordinary, no fire in the blocks or anything like that.'

'Leave the surveillance to us and don't leave the blocks any more. I'm arranging wagons for the sick who are still here. How many are there approximately?'

'Two thousand,' Hans said, exaggerating to make the business with the wagons more difficult than it already was.

'Fine, we'll come and get you at dawn.'

Back at disinfection the decision was soon made. They were going to break out. They split into three groups. One, led by Klempfner, would go to the building yard, where they knew of a bunker. The second group would hide near the town on the road to the camp, and the Spaniards would go to Raisko,* where they would have a view of the road that ran west along the Sola.† They were all more or less armed and, if discovered, would not surrender.

The Spaniards were the last to leave, with them Hans and Van den Heuvel, Hans's Dutch room orderly, who was allowed to go with them at his request. It was one a.m. They had cut the wires behind Block 28. On the watchtower was a prisoner, a member of the new camp police. Officially they were supposed to maintain order in the camp, but they actually stood watch on the towers and wandered the perimeter of the camp to make sure no dangerous groups of SS were approaching and that the coast was clear for those trying to flee.

Everything was safe. Apart from Krause, they hadn't seen any SS around at all. The soldiers at the gate weren't interested. Outside it was deathly quiet and fine, misty snow was sweeping over the camp. The lads were as stealthy as possible and spread out so that each one could just keep sight of the man ahead of him. At the front was Rudi, one of the Spanish Reds, who had worked in Raisko and knew the way well.

After half an hour they were in the village, which seemed completely deserted. They reached the small house Rudi had in mind. The door wasn't locked. They went inside and up the

* A sub-camp, which was part of a village, where vegetables, fruit and flowers were grown by prisoners.
† The river running south of Auschwitz.

stairs. Once they were all in the attic, Alfonso lit a small candle. The room was full of racks that were used in the nursery in the summer.

'I christen this house *"No Pasarán"*,' Alfonso said solemnly. No Pasarán – they shall not pass – the slogan of the Loyalists in the Spanish Civil War. And they all repeated it as a vow.

That night was damned cold. They had only brought a few blankets with them and didn't dare light a fire in the stove. For all they knew, there could still be some Jerries left in the village. Hans couldn't sleep from the cold. He kept thinking about Friedel and how she would be marching now, just marching the whole time, or maybe lying down somewhere in a barn or a factory. It could have all been so different. If Sara hadn't been too scared, they would be together now. They were relatively safe here. But Friedel . . . What a trek. No, he didn't want to think about it. He mustn't. Then he would fall asleep for a few minutes, only to wake again with a start whenever one of the lads made the slightest noise.

That night his fear gave rise to the vision that would take hold of him and not let go: the terrifying vision of Friedel in the snow. Sometimes she would be lying alone with a bullet wound in the back of her head, at other times she was buried under a pile of bodies. Sometimes she lay with a resigned smile on her face, as if a sweet memory of him had come to her in that final moment; at others her face was twisted with fear and horror. But always that one constant: Friedel in the snow.

He was overjoyed when day finally came and his companions – who were calm because they were so full of their approaching liberation and had mostly slept well – woke up too.

They looked out of the attic window at the small houses and, across the snowy fields, the large sawmills and the road that followed the river. Nowhere was there any sign of life. Nowhere was smoke curling up out of the chimneys. It was all completely deserted. Their own tracks had been snowed over and they felt safe.

The downstairs rooms were workshops with carpentry tools on the tables. They tossed them to one side and settled in a little, putting their baggage in the cupboard. Hans didn't have much with him: a tin box with some bandages and food, which he added to their combined reserves.

There was a good supply of briquettes in the cellar. For a moment they had a row about whether or not to risk a fire. The smoke would be visible for miles. But the longing for warmth won out over caution.

As the day progressed they felt more and more at ease. At first they only went outside to look for ice to melt for drinking water. But later they began scouting out the whole village, up to the abandoned camp where the girls who worked in the market garden had lived. They were beautiful barracks; the market garden had been a good Kommando.

Hans's spirits sank when he saw the mess hall, with bowls of soup still on the table and the small possessions the girls had been forced to abandon scattered over the floor: a skein of wool, a keepsake, a comb or a handkerchief. What had become of these girls? The vision rose in him again.

But this was no time for sentiment. They dragged straw mattresses back to the house, along with eating utensils and anything else they could find that was useful. The fire was burning well, they'd had a good meal and while one of them kept watch from the attic window, the others fell asleep on the mattresses in the warm room. They had enough blankets now and when exhaustion and comfort unite to invite sleep, even the most horrific and terrifying visions pale into a soft sheen of melancholy. Hans fell into a deep sleep that lasted many hours.

THE NEXT DAY WAS uneventful. Nobody appeared in the immense wilderness of snow. But on the third day they were shocked by a sudden pounding on the door. It was a Wehrmacht soldier. The lookout at the attic window hadn't seen him approaching. There was one blind corner and he must have come from that direction.

They consulted for a moment. 'Just let him in,' Alfonso said. They put on their caps to hide their shaven heads and opened the door. The soldier said hello and didn't seem the least suspicious.

How had they ended up in such a remote hideaway?

They told him they had been working on the other side of Krakow in a factory. They were foreign civilian workers. When the Russians came, they'd fled. They had walked for three days and were resting up here before continuing. The soldier took three of the lads with him. They had to help carry straw to the barracks, because a whole company was on its way.

Once the soldier was gone, Alfonso exploded at Nase, a Spanish Red. He was still wearing his prisoner's trousers: 'You fool, you could have given us all away! There were plenty of civvies to be found in the camp.' Fortunately one of the lads had a pair of civilian trousers to spare.

They lived together with the soldiers like that for a couple of days. Once, Alfonso and Rudi even went off with them in the lorry to pick up supplies from the SS canteen at the camp.

The lads got a share too. Tins of condensed milk, macaroni, preserves, meat and bottles of champagne. The SS still had plenty left over! They even brought back a saxophone they'd found there for Hans.

One afternoon a soldier came in who was a bit smarter than the rest. He began a story about some partisans they had been trying to hunt down and gave the lads a searching look. Hans started up a conversation with him to try to change the subject, but the soldier pointed at him. 'You look kind of Jewish. Take your caps off for a sec.' They were shocked and an awkward silence fell in the room. 'Ah, not that I give a stuff about that,' the soldier said, breaking the tension. 'I'm not like the damned SS!'

They could breathe again and Hans, who'd been in quite a stew about it, gave the soldier three tins of condensed milk. After he'd gone, the others all launched into Hans. Why hadn't he stayed in the background a little more? Why had he been so idiotic as to give the soldier milk, a childish attempt at bribery? As if that would restrain him if his intentions were bad.

Hans admitted that they were right. 'Of course, I'm no different from all those Jews in hiding in Holland who get caught and sent here. It's always a source of conflict. You have all kinds of Jews – intellectuals, who have never been involved in politics, as well as shopkeepers and hawkers who don't understand the situation at all – in hiding with the Dutch resistance. Because of their complete lack of political education and their difficult attitude, they often betray themselves and their hosts, and end up here. But I'll be more careful from now on.'

The soldiers left the same day. That evening, as it was getting dark, Jacques and Rudi went to the camp to see if there was any news. No, nothing special. The camp was completely unguarded and doing well because of it. Most of the people there were seriously ill, but there were enough Pfleger and healthy people hiding out there to keep it all turning over. There was just one thing: they had heard that there were still many thousands of women at Birkenau.

That news was especially interesting for Alfonso: 'Many thousands? How's that even possible? Birkenau was almost empty last week when the evacuation began, and some three thousand women left on the march. They went past our women's camp. Maybe women have come back from the transports after all. Maybe it's true that they've been cut off by the Russians. I'm going there tomorrow morning to have a look. I want to find out what it's really like there. You coming, Jacques?'

'Let me come too,' Hans asked. 'Maybe Friedel's there.'

'You? You'll just make a mess of things.'

Hans didn't answer. It would work out.

After much discussion Hans was allowed to go along. He had to do exactly what Alfonso said. He wasn't to split off from the others and if they bumped into any strangers on the way, he mustn't talk to them. He laughed, but wryly. They didn't have much faith left in his abilities as a partisan, but at least they were still taking him along. They knew how important it was to him.

The day had just dawned when they set out. Alfonso led the way. After a long discussion of the pros and cons, he'd left the submachine gun at home. They passed the women's barracks and came out in open fields. The snow was thirty centimetres deep, but that wasn't a problem for them in their boots and woollen socks.

After an hour they reached the railway line and could see the Birkenau barracks. When they came up to the camp gate, they saw a woman sitting in the snow against a post. The woman made a slow hand gesture. Hans squatted down next to her.

'Is it dinner time yet?' she asked, almost under her breath. Then she dozed off again. She must have been sitting there in the snow for a long time.

Jacques urged Hans to keep walking: 'Or maybe you want to help all the thousands lying in the snow?'

Jacques was right. They walked along the railway line that ran straight through this city of barracks, with the endless rows on either side of the line, everything white and deathly. Beside the railway line ran the road, the central Lagerstrasse, and there, along the road, lay the women, one every ten metres or so.

They were almost all old women, the weaker ones, who hadn't been able to keep up with the others right from the beginning of the death march, perhaps collapsing before it even began, during the hours of roll call. They were lying in bizarre poses. Hans had seen many dead bodies, but never such strange ones. Some had their arms wrapped around their legs, others were lying with one arm in the air, as if still trying to get up. But all of their heads were bloody. Their humane escorts had shot them all in the back of the head to put them out of their misery or, more accurately, to prevent any possibility of their being liberated by the Russians after all.

Many of the women were almost naked, the clothes pulled off their bodies by those who were closest. Not one was wearing shoes.

After they had walked about half a kilometre along the main road, they saw tracks in the snow curving off between two rows of barracks. They followed the tracks.

A few hundred metres further, they saw the first sign of life in the camp. A woman, a child still. When she saw the men, she fled into a barracks. They walked up to it and Alfonso pushed the door open. Their breath stopped short and their legs refused to take another step. The disgust that overcame them was like that of an invalid who feels the breath of death in the sickly sweet smell of chloroform. Hans held tight to the doorpost because this inferno with hundreds of pitiable beings, this warehouse with so many individuals, all dangling between life and death, made his head spin.

He couldn't take his eyes off the catastrophic living and the fortunate dead, lying jumbled together on the bunks. Accompanying all of this was quiet wailing and, when the men showed themselves, cries of fear and pleas for help. They braced themselves and went deeper into the barracks.

They spoke to the strongest of the women, who all told the same story. Six days ago the entire camp had been ordered to turn out. All the nurses and all of the sick who could make any kind of progress at all had been forced to go with them. The rest stayed in bed. Nobody gave them anything to eat, nobody nursed them, nobody took away the bodies. None of them had the strength for any of that. There were only a few of them who were able to go outside to relieve themselves. The others just did it in bed. The stench of faeces mixed with the smell of the corpses and the gases developing in black, frozen arms and legs ...

They spoke to a Czech girl. All these women were from Birkenau. No, she didn't know anything about transports that might have turned back. She herself had come here from Theresienstadt with her parents and sister. As the sisters were twins, the whole family was initially spared, because doing blood tests on twins was one of the Lagerarzt's hobbies. But then they'd lost track of their father, and their mother had died of dysentery two months ago. Now she was lying here with her sister in one bunk. Her sister had died last night. Before her death, she had asked her to turn her over so that she could look into her eyes one last time. With the two of them working together, they'd managed it. Today she would die too. She too was finished.

Hans swore. He thought of that family: the father, the mother, the two young girls . . . He saw them at home in Prague. It was summer and they'd gone for a walk. Then they'd sat down at an outdoor café for a refreshing drink. The father was talking about his business and the mother was praising him for having done his best and, after years of work, having fulfilled his dreams. And the sisters joked with each other when a boy from school passed and gave them a shy wave.

'So,' the father said, 'which of you two is the lucky one?'

They blushed and the whole family laughed.

And now the whole family had been destroyed. The last one was lying here with frozen feet waiting to die, weeping with her head pressed against her beautiful sister's body.

They went to the next barracks. Standing in the doorway was a man, a Hungarian.

'How did you get here?' Jacques asked.

The man was nervous. He turned around as if someone was threatening him from behind. Then he grabbed Jacques by the arm, let go of him, ran a hand over his head and looked back again. He gave an impression of total confusion. Then, in broken German: 'Last week we went on transport. Our troop was twelve hundred men. Terrible journey, walking day and night. I can walk, I was in a good Kommando, but so many exhausted. The first day at least one hundred dropped out. If they fell in snow, the SS counted to three, then fired. After one day we had walked forty kilometres. Then further again. One hundred kilometres in three days. There were only seven hundred of us left. All the roads of Upper Silesia are full of dead bodies. The night of the third day something was wrong. We were standing still and the SS were having a big discussion. It seemed our route was blocked by the Russians. We carried on along a forest road. It was a sunken road and the SS were walking on the sides, a few metres higher. Suddenly they started shooting. I dropped down next to a tree trunk. That saved me. After the SS left, I got up. Various others weren't dead. They were groaning softly but couldn't go on. They had been shot in the stomach or legs. With three of us we started on the way back. We hid in the daytime and walked at night. Sometimes the farmers gave us something to eat.'

'Was it like that with all the transports?' Hans asked.

'I don't know, but we won't see many of them again.'

No, he wasn't being left much hope. The vision was reality. It was strange that life still went on, that the Earth kept turning. We feel like we and our loved ones are the centre of the universe. But the universe doesn't care whether we're happy or die like dogs in the snow.

They went inside the second barracks. There Hans discovered a Dutch girl. She was called Adelheid and begged Hans to help her. He gave her a piece of bread he had in his pocket. She grabbed it like a starved animal and the women next to her raised themselves up on their elbows to get something too.

Hans promised this and promised that. What else could he do? But he knew he wouldn't keep his promises. He knew he couldn't help them. Even if he dragged everything he could find to these barracks, it wouldn't help, it would only cause fights and new misery. Because there were five more barracks like this one. Two thousand women lying on bunks between hundreds of dead bodies. Who could help here? The Russians? What was keeping them? Why wasn't the sound of artillery coming closer?

Of course, these two thousand unfortunates were just a fraction of the millions Berlin had on its conscience. But they were what was left of the greatest of all this war's calamities. They were the last coincidental letters written at the bottom of history's blackest page . . . 'Birkenau'.

It was evening by the time they got back to No Pasarán. They sat down by the stove, which was glowing red. Van den Heuvel was just making coffee when Alfonso, who was keeping watch, called out: 'A woman with a bandaged head.'

The lads crowded around the attic window and discussed what to do. The girl was a couple of hundred metres away and walking slowly – feeling her way, as it were – between the houses. In the gathering dusk they couldn't make out what kind of person she was, but the white bandage wrapped around her head stood out clearly.

'Let Jacques and Rudi go out to her,' Alfonso suggested. 'Be careful.'

'Fine, we'll go to the lookout tower first, then double back. That way our paths will cross.'

They set out. A few minutes later they were standing before her. The girl was shocked and asked in German who they were.

'Workers. From this area. Can we help you?'

For a moment she looked hesitantly at the men and then, leaning on a doorpost, she was unable to control herself any longer and burst out crying. Jacques put an arm around her and led her back to No Pasarán. When she saw the lads sitting around the stove with their shaven heads, she smiled through her tears. They gave her a place to sit near the stove and Van den Heuvel poured her a coffee. Max let fly at her right away.

'Where've you come from? How'd you get wounded like that?'

She flinched.

'Damn it, man, give her a bit of breathing space,' Hans snarled.

The girl looked at him.

'Are you from Holland?' she asked in Dutch.

Hans was very surprised and introduced himself.

'I remember you from Westerbork,' she replied. 'I'm Roosje . . . I was in the registration office.'

He laid a hand on her shoulder and told her to rest a little now.

'What happened to your head?'

'A blow with a gun butt. A farmer put a rough bandage on it for me.'

The bandage was no more than a strip torn from a bedsheet. Hans pulled out his tin box while Rudi unwrapped the old bandage. Roosje's hair was all clotted together with blood.

'How am I going to get this clean without hydrogen peroxide?'

'Just cut it off,' she said. 'It's full of lice anyway.'

Hans admired her pragmatism and reluctantly cut off her hair. Although the wound wasn't large, her scalp was split all the way through. She was in a lot of pain, but bore up bravely. After he'd dressed her wound, she lay down on the pile of mattresses. Everyone remained silent and drank their coffee.

Suddenly she began talking: 'I was in a labour camp near Neu Berun. I was there for four months with my mother and my little sister. My mother died last month.'

'When did you arrive from Westerbork?'

'We went to Theresienstadt six months ago. After that we were in Birkenau for a week and then we were sent on to the labour camp. There were a thousand of us: women aged between fourteen and sixty. Officially the limits were sixteen to fifty, but a lot of older women were scared and gave their ages as under fifty. First we lived in tents, but then, in November, the first snow fell and we got wooden huts. They were made for forty people, but they crammed a hundred of us into each one. That's how we got infected with lice and scabies.'

'How did they treat you?'

'It was hard labour. We were guarded by twenty men in black uniforms from the *SS Sonderdienst*. They had a political officer and an Oberscharführer, the '*Oscha*'. We were given three hundred grams of bread and a litre of soup a day. There was never anything extra and never anything we could organize. Two hundred died in four months. My mother too.'

'Wasn't there an infirmary?'

'Yes, there was a hospital tent. The Hungarian girls called it the "waiting room". You only went there when you were completely finished, to wait for death. Ah, we were all waiting for death. It was so awful.'

'Was there a doctor too?' Hans asked.

'Stop interrupting her,' Max snapped.

'When my mother died, we had to dig her grave ourselves. Never in my whole life have I felt so miserable. For Mother, death was a deliverance. She suffered dreadfully. She was always an intelligent woman, interested in all kinds of things, but towards the end she couldn't talk about anything but food. She had terrible diarrhoea and swollen legs. She worked until four days before she died. I don't understand how I can live on. My father dead, my mother too, and my sister gone.' She sighed and stopped telling her story for a moment.

'Where's your sister, then?' Alfonso asked.

'I don't know. We got separated. This is what happened: last week we saw the prisoners from Auschwitz marching on the roads. There were endless columns of them.'

'Were there many women among them?' Hans asked.

'Yes, but we weren't able to speak to anyone. Our guards kept us at a distance. We thought we would be leaving soon too, but we had to work until the day before yesterday. I think they kept us at it for so long because we were digging tank traps. Early yesterday morning it was suddenly: "All fall in." Only the sick and the women who didn't have any shoes had to stay behind. Altogether that was more than two hundred because a lot of women had worn out their shoes so badly they'd had to work in the snow in their bare feet. Five hundred women marched off. I don't know what happened to them. Those of us who stayed behind were expecting death.' She fell silent and bit her lip.

'Why can't you tell us any more?' Hans asked.

'You won't believe me.'

'Why not? We know all too well that the SS is capable of anything. Back in Holland, I didn't want to believe what they were saying on the BBC about Polish Jews being gassed. Now, unfortunately, we know better.'

She shrugged: 'In Holland, they won't believe us either when we go back and tell them everything.'

'So we'll make ourselves believable and official reports that prove the truth of our stories will be published. And if somebody still refuses to believe it, I'll just ask them where my mother and father are. Where are my brothers and all the tens of thousands of others . . .'

'Maybe you're right, doctor . . . After the big group had marched off, we were left with two hundred women, the Oscha and two guards. Then the Oscha went into two blocks to give all of the women an injection. The injection was supposedly for typhoid fever and had to be given intravenously. But we understood all too well what those injections were for. The Oscha didn't give the injections properly in the veins and because of that it only killed two girls. They couldn't speak any more and died in a confused state a couple of hours later. The Oscha mustn't have had enough of the liquid because he only injected about fifty women. In the afternoon he came into the blocks with the two Sturmmänner and had all those who could still move line up outside. It was a miserable troop of a hundred half-dressed women, barefoot in the snow. Most of them had blankets wrapped around them. They only had one wish: to suffer as little as possible. No traces of fear were visible in their hollow faces. They all knew what it was about. They had all seen it coming, for four long months. Enough of hunger, enough of cold, wounds, lice and scabies.'

'But didn't you realize how close the Russians were? Didn't you have any possibility of saving yourselves, of resisting? There were only three SS men, after all.' It was Alfonso, the fiery Spaniard, the fighter from the Civil War who had fought hard for life. He threw the words at her feet as a protest against what seemed to him unthinkable cowardice.

She smiled at his outburst. 'Oh, several walked off, but most of them could hardly put one foot in front of the other, they were so emaciated. No, death didn't come as an enemy, but as the saviour. A Hungarian girl – Judith was her name – was crying. The Oscha shoved her in the chest: "Don't cry, you silly goose."

"What are you going to do with us, Oscha?"

"I'm going to kill you all."

"But I want to see my parents again so much."

"You'll see them – in the next world."

'Then the troop set off. Slowly, step by step, leaning on each other and shuffling along. We were going to the tank trap we ourselves had dug. It was three hundred metres away. That took us almost half an hour. There was always someone trying to run off, but mostly the Oscha caught up to her easily. Still, some managed to get away.

'Halfway I nudged my sister. "We have to try," I said. She didn't want to. She didn't feel capable of making another effort. But when the Oscha was chasing an old woman who had got some fifty metres away, and the guards were on the other side of the row watching, I pulled my sister along behind me and we ran as best we could.

'But our torturer came back too soon and set out after us. We had a head start of a hundred metres at most. Anja could hardly take another step. There was only one chance. I called out to Anja to let herself drop. She rolled into a ditch and I ran on as fast as I could. The Oscha didn't bother about Anja and came after me. It was the hardest moment of my life. I was completely exhausted.'

She was silent for a moment. Tears welled up in her eyes. 'Then I surrendered and walked back with the Oscha. We came to the pits and everyone had to lie down on their stomachs. The SS men fired three volleys from their machine guns. I was still alive, but driven half mad and only wanting one thing: "Oh God, let me die." I couldn't take it any more. And then the three men were there, finishing off the job, bringing the butts of their guns down on their victims' heads. I can still see the blood splattering around and the women, the three men and the white snow, all turning red. Then they hit me too and it was all over.'

The girl sighed deeply.

Jacques gently stroked her arm. She smiled for a moment, as if relieved, as if happy that she had now been able to unburden her heart to trusted comrades.

'They'd done their work badly. After a short time, maybe an hour, I regained consciousness. I was lying in the pit among the murdered women, but I was still alive. Then I felt that something had changed inside of me. I had to stay alive. I wanted to live to tell all of this, to tell everyone about it, to convince people that it was true . . . to take revenge for my mother, revenge for my fiancé and for all the millions who have been murdered. There are variations on the theme – gassing, hanging, drowning, starving and more – but I had survived one of those. I had seen death and lived to tell the tale. I have to tell it, and I will tell it.'

Again she was silent and looked at the lads. They sat quietly with grim faces and listened to the roar of artillery.

'Ten kilometres,' Jacques said and they gritted their teeth. Another ten kilometres and they would be free. No, not free, because they had a task, a purpose in life that bound them. They had to shout out what they had experienced. They felt that they were the apostles of a vengeance so thorough that barbarism would be exterminated on Earth for ever, a vengeance that would purify the world and open it up to a new humanism.

'I was half frozen and I had a terrible headache, but I managed to get out of the pit. I stumbled to the place where Anja had dropped to the ground. She wasn't there any more, but I could see her tracks leading away through the snow and believed she had saved herself. I staggered on to the barracks. Lying inside were the bodies of the women who hadn't been able to walk and must have been dealt with after us. When I went into Block 8, the typhoid block, savage joy flowed through me. The block was alive. Like everywhere, they hadn't completed their work here either. The Oscha must have really meant it that morning when he'd said: "Those typhoid sufferers will die by themselves!" I lay down on the straw and went to sleep. Around nightfall we experienced another great shock: the Wehrmacht! But the soldiers didn't harm us. On the contrary. They emptied out the camp stores and gave us food and some clothes. When it was properly dark, I left. I wanted to go to Birkenau because I thought that Anja would have gone in that direction too, in hope of finding her husband. It was a harsh trek through the snow and by morning I was hopelessly lost. A farmer took me in, bandaged me and gave me something to eat. I slept all day. Around nightfall I set out again, and now . . .'

They had the impression that the danger from the SS really was over and that, in the final hours and the fighting that would now come, the camp might be more likely to be spared than an abandoned village. Accordingly several of the lads went back to the camp. In the ward they looked at Hans as if he were a ghost. Japie, the small Dutch room orderly, was overjoyed. He had been terrified the whole time.

Hans sat down next to Gedl, an engineer.

'You were right, son, to get out of here.'

'Why's that?' Hans asked.

'Haven't you heard what happened here yesterday? At three in the afternoon a squad of SS men turned up, those dogs from the extermination Kommando, dressed in black and armed to the teeth. They came into the blocks and chased everybody out with the butts of their rifles. Poor old Zlobinsky got a cracked skull out of it. Even the most severely ill were out on the street. They were being held up by the Pfleger and the other patients who could still walk. Then they told us we could go back inside again. They were going to get lorries to take us to the train and when they came back and gave us the order, we had to fall in immediately. After that they went to Birkenau and got up to the same tricks all over again. A lot of the people there couldn't even get out of bed. With about a thousand sick people from Birkenau, they started marching towards Auschwitz. They were just a few hundred metres outside the camp when a lorry came. They called out something. The SS men jumped into the back of the lorry, and since then we haven't seen hide nor hair of them. Most of the people went back to Birkenau. Some of the ones who could walk a bit better carried on to Auschwitz.'

'Do you know what they called out from the lorry?'

'According to people who were standing close by, "*Der Zug ist schon da.*" A train was supposed to come at seven o'clock to take all the SS from this district to safety. The train came a few hours early and saved all our lives.'

'Are you sure they wanted to kill everyone?'

Gedl sent Japie upstairs to get someone. It was a small man. Although he looked terrible, there was still something determined about the way he held himself.

'Dr Weill from Slovakia.'

Hans shook his hand. 'You should be home soon.'

'Home is a relative concept. My whole family has been wiped out here. Anyway, yesterday I escaped by the skin of my teeth. I was a doctor in Trzebinia, a mining Kommando thirty kilometres from here. They marched off six hundred men. I was left behind with ninety men, almost all sick. Yesterday about midday an SS squad came, twelve men. They had everyone who could walk line up in front of the barracks. Then, in the space of a few minutes, they killed all of the patients who had stayed in bed with revolver shots. There were about forty of us who could walk. We had to build a pyre of straw mattresses and lay the bodies on it – a layer of straw mattresses, then a layer of bodies – and every time we came out of the barracks with another load, they kept about ten of us back and shot them too. Three times an SS man asked me: "Aren't you tired yet, doctor?" Why I kept saying no, I don't know. None of it made any difference. Anyway, I was carrying the last bodies out of the barracks when a man in plain clothes came up to me. I knew him; he was a Gestapo supervisor from the mine. I had organized medicine for him sometimes. "Don't you want to climb over that wire, doctor?" I thought he was mocking me, but what did I have to lose? Miracle of miracles, he was serious. They let me escape.'

'Yes, son,' Gedl added, 'the SS men who came here an hour later were the same ones. You understand what would have become of us. Fortunately the heroes were more concerned with getting the train out of here than doing their "duty" with regard to us. We're all alive thanks to a chain of miracles.'

'We need sugar, otherwise I can't make pancakes,' Japie insisted. Hans had seen sugar somewhere. He thought it was in Block 14 and headed off with a bag.

In Block 14 there was nothing to be found. He went to Block 13 and down to the cellar where three men were sitting calmly smoking as if nothing was going on. Hans said hello and asked them if they'd seen any sugar. The oldest smiled: 'We haven't seen anything here at all. We only came here from Birkenau yesterday.' He spoke very poor German.

Hans asked him where he was from and if he maybe preferred to speak French. That made conversation easier. The man introduced himself as Kabeli or, rather, Professor Kabeli – he was a professor at the faculty of literature in Athens. Hans sat down with them and asked which Kommando the professor had worked in.

'Sonderkommando.'

Hans was startled. It was the first time he had met someone who had worked in the gas chambers and crematoria.

Now that everything was over, he would hear exactly what had happened in Birkenau.

The professor smiled: 'You don't dare to ask anything, but I don't find it at all unpleasant to tell people about it. After all, when you get back to Holland you'll have to be able to inform them precisely.'

'Were you in the Sonderkommando for a long time?'

'A year. In general you only survived two to three months, but I had protection and because of that I was able to slip through.'

'Would you like to tell me something about the crematoria?'

'Certainly. There were four crematoria. One and Two were near the train, Three and Four in the pine forest behind the *Zigeunerlager* – that's the far north corner of the camp. I worked in Crematoria Three and Four with a lot of Greeks. Let me do a sketch of Crematorium Three.

'Seven hundred to one thousand people arrived in one go. All kinds came mixed up together: men, women and children, infants and old people, sick and healthy. Mostly the strong young men and women were picked out at the train to be interned as slave labourers, but often the entire transport was sent straight to the crematorium.

'The people came into Waiting Room A and then through a narrow hall into Room B, where there were all kinds of slogans about hygiene on the walls. Things like *"Halte dich sauber"* and *"Vergesse nicht deine Seife"* to maintain until the last moment the illusion that the people were going to have a shower. Room B was where they had to get undressed. In each of the four corners there was an SS man with a machine gun. But they never needed to use them, the people were all calm. Even those who understood that they were going to their deaths felt how pointless it was to resist, and if fighting death is futile, then let the suffering be as brief as possible.

'Sometimes – when many transports arrived one after the other – things had to be done in a hurry. Then the Sonderkommando was put to work and had to cut people's clothes off their bodies, rip watches off arms and tear jewellery off fingers. Long hair was cut off because it had industrial value. Then the whole troop was sent into the "showers". That was a large room with artificial lighting. In the ceiling there were three rows of shower heads. Once all the people were inside, the big door slammed shut. It was electrically operated and had rubber on the edges that sealed it off, airtight. Then it was time for the final act. The gas was in tins, and in those tins there were grains as big as peas, probably crystals of the condensed gas ethane cyanide – "Cyclone". In the ceiling there were holes between the showers. The SS men emptied their tins through those holes and then quickly closed them again. The gas was released and five minutes later it was all over. Many of the victims would have never been aware of what was happening to them, but those who realized often tried to hold their breath and died in contortions.

'Sometimes it was different: I remember how one day two hundred and fifty Polish-Jewish children were going to be gassed. After they had undressed they formed a long line of their own accord and, singing "Sh'ma Yisrael", the Jewish prayer of the dying,* they entered the gas chamber with perfect discipline.

---

* Otherwise known as 'The Shema', this prayer is a centrepiece of daily morning and evening prayer and considered by some to be the most essential prayer in Judaism. It is also usual to recite it before bedtime and when death is imminent.

'The SS man would keep an eye on his watch: the hatches had to be kept shut for five minutes. Then he pressed a button and on both sides of the gas chamber the row of hatches opened electrically. When enough of the gas had drifted out, the Sonderkommando went into the gas chamber. They carried long poles with hooks on the end. The hooks were placed around the necks of the victims, who were then dragged to the crematorium, which you can see indicated on the sketch with D.

'There were four furnaces, and four bodies went into each furnace at once. The big iron doors opened, the trollies rolled out. The bodies went on top and they slid the trollies back in. The doors closed and fifteen minutes later it was all over. With four furnaces like that, a crematorium could process a lot. But sometimes it still wasn't fast enough. The SS knew what to do then too. Two big ditches had been dug behind the crematorium, as you can see here: thirty metres long, six metres wide and three metres deep. In the bottom, big tree trunks with petrol poured over them. That made an immense fire that people could see from kilometres away.

'One of those ditches could take a thousand bodies at once. The incineration took twenty-four hours, then the ditches were ready for a new load. Everything was taken into account. There was also drainage. A trench ran from the ditches to a small ravine twenty or thirty metres away. The burning mass ran down through those trenches into the ravine. I assure you that I have seen with my own eyes how a man who was working near the pyre got down into the trench to dip his bread into the molten, flowing human fat. You just have to be hungry.

'On 5 June 1944 a special Hungarian children's transport arrived. As so often in a period with a lot of big transports, the gentlemen from the SS didn't even have the patience to wait a proper five minutes for the gas to take effect. As a result we had to throw the children into the ditch while they were still half alive. A Greek, Lotsi Mordechai, couldn't take it any more and threw himself into the ditch. A lot of the others had had enough too. Alexander Hereirra, also a Greek, with an athletic build, agreed with three Poles and six Russians that they would destroy Crematoria Three and Four. A few days after Lotsi Mordechai's suicide, Hereirra beat the SS sergeant to death with a shovel. Their plan came to nothing. Hereirra was killed and his body was put on display that evening at roll call in *D-Lager*, where all of the Kommandos who were involved in the exterminations were housed. Still, Crematorium Three didn't exist much longer. On 2 October 1944 the uprising took place.

'There was a conspiracy between the 243 Greeks and the other nationalities in the Sonderkommando. They had managed to organize a machine gun with two thousand bullets from the Auto Union factory. Petrol, they had in abundance. They attacked the SS guards and overcame them. They set fire to the crematorium and killed the sentries at the fence. Unfortunately hundreds got frightened at the last minute and didn't join in. In ten minutes the Birkenau SS was fully mobilized. SS troops from Auschwitz were brought in too and our men, who were already past the fence, were surrounded. Twenty-five were killed immediately, the rest were burnt the next day along with twenty men from each Kommando working around the crematoria. The Poles betrayed the names of the uprising's organizers.

I'm proud that they were Greeks. Five heroes: Baruch, Burdo, Carasso, Ardite and Jachon.

'The last "commissions" were on 24 October. On 12 December 1944 they began demolishing the crematoria. Twenty-five men – Greeks, Poles and Hungarians from the Sonderkommando – were assigned to work on the demolition. I was one of them. None of the others who lived in D-Lager were left. We were the last ones in the whole Lager. That was how we came to be forgotten during the evacuation and how I can now tell you all this.'

'How will we ever be able to make them pay for it?' remarked one of the others after a long silence.

'Nothing will make up for it,' Hans said. 'All we can do is exterminate all of that SS scum.'

'So you think it's just the responsibility of the SS or, rather, the party?' Kabeli asked. 'Are the rest of that nation angels?'

'Definitely not,' Hans admitted. 'The entire German nation is responsible. They're losing the war now and will renounce their leaders, but if they'd won the war, nobody would ever have asked the Führer which means he had used or what had happened to all of the Communists and Jews.'

'So should the whole German nation be gassed as a punishment?'

'No, Sir, definitely not, but everyone who was part of the SS, the Gestapo and so on will need to be wiped out to make sure they never come back. The rest of the German nation needs to be kept under foreign control until a new generation has grown up with a humanist education and upbringing, and removed from the militaristic influence of big business and the nobility. Then, maybe after many years, a socialist German nation might be able to live independently.'

The next morning bullets ticked against the walls of the blocks. It was mysterious; there were no soldiers in sight. Hans was helping in the Block 21 outpatients on the camp's southern corner, near the Sola.

Then an enormous bang. Plaster fell from the ceiling and several windows shattered. He looked out. The river was flowing fast, swollen from the thaw. And there, floating among the chunks of ice, were beams and planks – what was left of the bridge.

'They've blown the bridge.'

They realized now that it was all over. The Germans were trying to delay the Russian pursuit, but their main force must have already been many kilometres away.

The camp was out of danger. Without noticing it, they had already spent a whole day in no-man's-land. A couple of hours later, the first Russians came strolling up in their white camouflage suits as if it were nothing out of the ordinary. Walking in the middle of the road as if no Germans existed. When they saw the prisoners in their uniforms, they smiled silently, no doubt thinking of their parents, who had been murdered by the Germans; their wives, who had been raped; their country, that had been turned into a wasteland. And the prisoners thought of their wives and children, of all the people they would never see again.

There was a long, grateful handshake, but no cheers escaped their throats, which were choked with emotion.

Now everything was different. Now the dream had become reality. In many places the wire had been cut and posts had been knocked over, and in those places there was a brisk traffic of lorries and horse-drawn wagons going in and out of the camp. It was beautiful, radiant weather, the sun was shining with new vigour, everywhere clumps of snow were falling from the rooftops. It was as if Nature wanted to add her bit to make the promise of new life complete. Hans couldn't bear it in the camp any longer. An inner tension was forcing him to take flight, like a bird whose cage has just been opened.

He walked in the direction of Raisko. The roar of guns faded; the tumult of war had receded into the distance, where the Germans were trying to form a new front. After a short while he reached No Pasarán. He was shocked by the state of the village. The house had been partly destroyed by a shell. Close to it were two German tanks that had probably caused this havoc. One was completely burnt out.

Hans went into the small house. There was nobody there. The living room was intact, but the kitchen was a ruin. There he found the remnants of the saxophone. He had to smile. What could material loss mean now?

Still, he was nervous. It was as if something was driving him to start walking again, further and further, to an unknown goal. Or to keep walking until, overcome by exhaustion, he lay down on the side of the road until it was all over.

He walked across fields that were still covered with snow. It had been reduced to a thin layer, and now and then he stepped in a puddle. His feet were wet, and despite the warmth of the sun he felt cold and uncomfortable.

Suddenly he was standing in front of the tower. He didn't know how he had ended up there. He hadn't been looking for the tower at all. He'd just wandered through the fields aimlessly, without a goal. The wood was wet and still covered in snow here and there. He climbed up cautiously.

The tower had three platforms. After reaching the first, he looked down. He felt extremely uneasy: fear of heights. Again he felt that 'something' was compelling him to move. Not away now, not far away until fatigue had drained his last bit of strength, but down. One false step and he would be lying there, broken but free of the sorrow that gripped him, together with her who filled his thoughts.

But he forced himself to keep going up. He had to, he couldn't give in, he had to stand up to the pressure. He couldn't flee, he had to fight. He had to keep on fighting, always. 'Alone we are none,' he had written. It was poetry. Life went on. The blood flowing through his veins forced him on, and if he insisted on going higher his legs would not refuse to carry him. So he kept climbing. A little unsteadily at first, but then determinedly, step after step.

Above the last step there was a hatch. He pushed it open and climbed up on to the highest platform. He felt a sense of victory. Victory over death. Now he was standing high above all the trees and houses. He felt like he could smell the spring in the gentle breeze caressing his head.

Not far away was the camp. From here he could see the holes that had been smashed in the white wall. Again he felt like a victor, so high up and looking out over the camp he was never meant to escape.

A little to the left lay Birkenau. It was enormous. Even from up here, where he had the whole world at his feet, where there seemed to be no limit to how far his gaze extended, Birkenau looked big. It had been big. A work of demonic magnitude had been carried out there. In that place more people had been killed than anywhere else in the world. It had been run according to an extermination system of incomparable perfection. But it hadn't been absolutely perfect. Otherwise he wouldn't have been able to stand here; he wouldn't have been alive. Why was he alive? What gave him the right to live? In what way was he better than all those millions who had died?

Not sharing the fate of all those others felt like an unfathomable evil. But he thought of what the girl in No Pasarán had said: 'I have to stay alive to tell all of this, to tell everyone about it, to convince people that it was true . . .'

His gaze wandered to the south. The still-snowy fields stretched out in the sharp light of early spring. But there in the south the horizon was not an infinity, he couldn't see an immense distance. In that direction, his gaze came up against a barrier.

To the south his horizon was blocked by the Beskid Mountains and there was that vision again: 'Friedel'. He gripped the railing, his fingers trying to dig into the wood, just as she had once gripped the mesh on the windows of Block 10. Then they had looked out over the distant fields together. Now they were separated. He was here and she was there, where the vision drew her, as if the silhouette on the horizon was not the outline of the mountains but the shape of her body.

The whole world was open to him now, but that was somewhere he would never go, somewhere that was now eternally unattainable. Once they had stood alongside each other and the longing in their hearts had carried them away to those mountains. Now she was gone, as out of reach as those faraway mountains had once been.

Now he was alone.

But not entirely. Because he still had her image before him. Inside him this vision would stay alive for ever. He would draw strength from it for what had become his task in life. She would exist through him so that her life would not have been in vain, and her soul would live through him, even if her body was resting there in those hazy blue mountains.

*D*URING THE POST-LIBERATION MONTHS, *Eddy had no idea if Friedel was still alive.*

At first he was convinced that she was dead, that she must have died on the death march that had taken her away from him at Auschwitz. As the stories of the death marches trickled through, he heard that there were survivors and regained hope.

Through the work of the Red Cross in Europe after the war, Eddy and Friedel were reunited in the Netherlands on 24 July 1945.

Glossary

Achtung! Attention!

Achtung, Lagerarzt! Attention, the camp doctor!

Alles aufstehen! Everyone, get up!

Alte Kamp-Insassen Dutch-German term used at Westerbork for senior inmates

Alter Häftling Senior prisoner, a prisoner who has been an inmate for a long time

Ältester Literally, elder. A term used in combination with an area specification to indicate the senior or head prisoner in a camp, block or room

Ambulanz Outpatients

Appel vorbei Roll call over

Arbeit macht frei Work sets you free

Arbeit macht frei ... Krematorium drei! Work sets you free ... Crematorium Three!

Arbeitslager Labour camp

Arztvormelder, antreten! Those presenting to the doctor, line up!

Aufgehen! Broken or corrupted German: March!

Aufnahme Admissions

Aufseherin Female overseer

Bademeister Washroom supervisor

Bauhof Building yard

Bekleidungskammer Warehouse for prisoner clothing

Berufsverbrecher Professional criminal

Bewegung Movement

Bewegung, Bewegung, los, Eile! Movement, movement, go, hurry!

Birkenallee Birch Avenue

Block Word used for the main buildings housing prisoners at Auschwitz and other German camps

Blockältester Block senior, a prisoner in charge of a block

Blockführerstube The guardhouse of the SS block overseer

Blockschonung Block rest, permission to remain in barracks and rest, granted to those unfit to work but not sick enough for hospital

Blöd Stupid

Blöde The stupid ones

Blöde Holländer Stupid Dutchman

Blöde Sauen Stupid pigs (Literally, sows)

Blödes Schwein Stupid pig

Bunkier The Auschwitz camp jail in the cellar of Block 11

Canada Nickname for the section of Auschwitz where the warehouses were located

Dalej! Polish: Go on!

Davai, bystro! Russian: Come on, faster!

DAW Short for *Deutsche Ausrüstungswerkstatte*, the German Equipping Workshops

Der Zug ist schon da The train has already come

Die Juden sind unser Unglück The Jews are our misfortune

Distrikt Krakau District of Krakow

Du Dreckhund You filthy dog

Du Drecksau You filthy pig

Du Idiot You idiot

Effektenkammer Warehouse for items taken from prisoners on their arrival

Eile Hurry

Eintritt verboten No entry

Ein Vogel Literally, a bird, but here meaning a peculiarity or strange habit

Es lebe Polen! Poland for ever!

Faulgas Marsh gas, also name of a *Kommando* working on a marsh gas plant

FKL Short for *Frauenkonzentrationslager*, women's concentration camp

Flying Column Dutch: *Vliegende Kolonne*. In Westerbork a group of prisoners that had to carry out special tasks that needed to be done quickly

Frauenkonzentrationslager Women's concentration camp

Frech Impudent or cheeky

Gespritzt Injected

Häftling Prisoner

Häftling 27903 mit 15 Häftlingen zur Strassenbau Prisoner 27903 with fifteen prisoners for roadworks

Häftlingskrankenbau Prisoners' Hospital

Häftlingsnummer Prisoner number

Hals-Nasen-Ohrenarzt Ear, nose and throat doctor

Halt Stop

Halt's Maul Shut up

Halte dich sauber Keep clean

Hau ruck! Pull!

Heilkräutertee Herbal tea

Herrgott Sakrament, verflucht noch mal God almighty, damn it

Himmel, Arsch und Zwirn, Herr Gott Sakrament, du verfluchter Idiot For God's sake, Christ Almighty, you cursed idiot

Hitler verrecke! Death to Hitler!

Hygienisch-bakteriologischen Untersuchungsstelle der Waffen-SS und Polizei Südost Hygienic-Bacteriological Research Centre of the Waffen SS and Police, South East

Interne Abteilung Internal Department

Judenblut spritzt vom Messer Jewish blood is dripping from the knives

Kapo A prisoner who oversaw other prisoners in work details

Kesselkommando Kettle-carrying detail

Kolkhoz Russian: A collective farm

Kommandantur Camp commandant's office

Kommando A work detail or squad

Kommandoführer SS overseer of a work detail

Krakauer Zeitung A Krakow newspaper

Krankenbau Hospital (in Auschwitz, the *Krankenbau* was spread out over several blocks)

KZ Short for *Konzentrationslager*, concentration camp

Lager Camp, also used as an administrative unit for subdivisions within a larger camp

Lagerältester Camp senior, the camp's head prisoner. As the term *Lager* – camp – was also used for subdivisions within Auschwitz and Birkenau, there was more than one *Lagerältester*

Lagerarzt Camp doctor (an SS medical officer). As the term *Lager* – camp – was also used for subdivisions within Auschwitz and Birkenau, there was more than one *Lagerarzt*

Lagerfriseur Camp barber

Lagerführer SS officer in charge of the camp

Lagerstrasse Camp street

Lagersuppe Camp soup

Le professeur hollandais French: The Dutch professor

Los! Go!

Los, Schweinehunde! Move it, you swine! (Literally, pig-dogs)

Mussulman Muslim, camp slang for a prisoner in an extreme state of physical and mental exhaustion

Nebellager Short for *Nacht und Nebellager*, camps where prisoners were held and executed in secret

No Pasarán Spanish: They shall not pass, Republican rallying cry in the Spanish Civil War

Oberscharführer SS rank: senior squad leader

Obersturmführer SS rank: senior assault leader

Operationssaal Operating theatre

Oscha Short for *Oberscharführer*, senior squad leader

Pfleger Nurse, used to designate a general assistant's job held by prisoners in the camp hospitals. Not all *Pfleger* had medical qualifications and most of their duties were non-medical

Pflegerstube Nurses' room

Prämienschein Bonus token

Prominent (noun) A privileged prisoner

Rapportführer SS officer in charge of roll calls

Rassenschande Racial outrage, a violation of Nazi laws prohibiting sexual contact between 'races'

Rein Clean

Reinlichkeit ist der Weg zur Gesundheit Cleanliness is the path to health

Reservepfleger Reserve nurse: a prisoner who has been approved as a *Pfleger* but is waiting to be appointed to a block

Röntgenraum X-ray room

Rotspanier Spanish Reds, term for Germans who fought for the Republicans in the Spanish Civil War

Rottenführer SS rank: section leader

Sanitäter Orderly

Sanitätslager der Waffen-SS Waffen SS Medical Supply Centre

Sauberkeit ist der halbe Weg zur Gesundheit Cleanliness is halfway to health

Scharführer SS rank: squad leader

Scheisse, Arzt Shit, doctor

Scheissmeister Latrine supervisor

Schnell! Los! Tempo! Quick! Go! Fast!

Schreibstube Office

Schulungslager Training camp

Schutzhäftling Prisoner in protective custody

SDG Short for *Sanitätsdienstgrad*, SS medical orderly

Selection Camp term for the selection of prisoners for extermination

Sonderkommando Special detail, prisoners who worked in the gas chambers and crematoria

SS-Krankenrevier SS hospital

SS-Revier Short for *SS-Krankenrevier*, SS hospital

SS Sonderdienst A Nazi paramilitary formation in occupied Poland

SS-Standortverwaltung Süd-Ost SS Local Administration South East

Standgericht Military court

Standortarzt Doctor for the SS garrison

Stehbunker Standing bunker

Stój Polish: Stop

Strafkommando Punishment detail

Stubenältester A prisoner in charge of a room

Sturmbannführer SS rank: assault unit leader

Sturmmann SS rank: storm trooper

Transport The deportation or movement of a group of Jews or other prisoners

Très charmant French: Very charming

Übermensch A superman, used here ironically to indicate a Nazi fantasy of the superior Aryan

Überstellung Strafkommando Birkenau Transfer to the Birkenau punishment detail

Unterscharführer SS rank: junior squad leader

Vergesse nicht deine Seife Don't forget your soap

WA Short for Dutch: *Weerbaarheidsafdeling*, the paramilitary wing of the NSB, the Dutch National Socialist party

Was ist hier los, ihr Dreckhuren! What's going on here, you filthy whores!

Wiener Blut Viennese spirit

Wir fahren gegen Engeland We are sailing against England

Zigeunerlager Gypsy camp, part of Birkenau concentration camp

Zivilarbeiter Civilian worker

Zum Befehl At your command

Zwischen Nacht und Nebel Literally, between night and fog

Afterword
by John Boyne

WITH EACH NEWLY PUBLISHED memoir, history book or novel that details the crimes that took place across Europe during the Holocaust, our understanding of that period increases in direct correlation with our dismay at the brutality of our species. Some of the most important writers of the last seventy-five years have shared their experiences of the camps in print, but, to the best of our knowledge, Eddy de Wind's *Last Stop Auschwitz* is the only book written from within a concentration camp itself. Because of this, it offers a unique insight into a tragedy that, more than any other event, defines the twentieth century and drapes it in infamy.

I've read many autobiographies centred around life and death within Auschwitz, Dachau, Treblinka and the dozens of other death camps, and each time I've found myself aston-ished by how deeply the daily events of camp life emblazoned themselves on the minds of the survivors, scorched into their collective memories with as much indiscriminate savagery as the tattoos carved into their arms. From the naive perspective of historical distance, one imagines that those who left the camps with their lives would do all they could to forget what they had been through – but no, it seems that memory can prove the most unwelcome consequence of trauma and that testimony is its necessary antidote.

Eddy de Wind's memoir represents a singular addition to the wealth of material that readers, historians and scholars can access as they try to comprehend the incomprehensible. While images of Jews 'standing stark-naked in the burning sun', as barbers 'with their blunt razors . . . tore out the hair more than shaving it off', are familiar to students of the subject, there's something visceral about reading the words from a man who both suffered these indignities and determined to write about them. One wonders how he felt transferring those recollections from mind to page, whether they served to relieve or relive those dark days.

De Wind's descriptions of the people and experiences that populated Auschwitz – the prisoners, the guards, the fences, the food, the tattoos, the showers and the slaughter – offer a rich insight into a man who was watchful while being watched and who, perhaps without even intending to, stored his memories away for the moment when the world would defeat the Nazis; their crimes would need to be exposed if they were to be prevented from happening again. The service he and so many other writers of this period have done for us is not quantifiable.

As with all memoirs of life in the camps, one turns the pages with a growing sense of disillusionment in mankind. It's impossible for the reader not to question what he or she might have done if subjected to such tortures, or, indeed, if asked to take part in them. Descriptions of the corpse carriers jumping out of the way to keep their clothes clean as they threw the bodies of the dead into the back of a lorry are among the many subtle and horrific insights that the author draws upon, along with 'enormous stacks of tins: the urns of the Poles whose bodies had been burnt there', and the sound of executions at seven o'clock at night: 'First the order to fire, then a volley, then the bodies being dragged away. And it kept on going like that. And then the cries of the victims. A girl begging for mercy because she was still so young and so desperate to live.'

One of the most tormenting experiences that is so well depicted in *Last Stop Auschwitz* is how painful was the separation of loved ones, and when the narrator's thoughts turn so often to his wife Friedel, one can understand his constant dread of what might be happening to her and his uncertainty about whether they would ever be reunited. While the closing pages of this memoir are painful in their descriptions of grief, this book serves as a testament to her life.

'Practised in hate, the SS was an organ for the oppression of their own German people and related nations,' de Wind writes. 'They rehearsed their methods on the Jews, Russians and Gypsies under the motto of racial purification . . . In the camps, the members of the SS were able to satisfy the sadistic tendencies that had been aroused in them, and because they were given these opportunities of satisfaction, they remained obedient followers of Hitler until the end.'

It's an extraordinary case to make and one that challenges us to question whether evil is an incarnate element of the human experience, a malevolence that lies dormant within each of us, which can be awoken at any time if we do not remain vigilant against the forces that still threaten the world three-quarters of a century after the end of the Second World War.

This is only one of the many moments of great insight that mark this memoir out as something valuable. When the Slovakian doctor mentions that 'Home is a relative concept. My whole family has been wiped out here,' the reader is surprised to realize that the prospect of liberation from the camps might have provoked mixed feelings in the inmates. Naturally, from the moment of arrival, each man, woman and child would have wanted to return to the cities and towns from which they had been taken, but the prospect of returning alone, of going back to a place and time that had been so changed by loss and poisoned by trauma, must have caused unexpected dread. It's no wonder that so many of those who managed to survive the war found themselves experiencing such guilt about being among the living that they were unable to continue. Perhaps the word 'survivor' is itself a misnomer.

As this book is published, some of those who were in the camps as children or young people are still alive to tell their stories. Soon, they too will be part of history, and both we and future generations will rely on narratives like *Last Stop Auschwitz* to guide our memories and stand as a testimony to those who died. In the literature, we continue to remember the lost millions who achieve immortality through the work of writers such as Eddy de Wind.

John Boyne
September 2019

A Note on the Author
and the Text

Hᴏᴡ ᴅɪᴅ Eᴅᴅʏ ᴀɴᴅ Fʀɪᴇᴅᴇʟ end up in Westerbork? What were Eddy's experiences after the Red Army liberated Auschwitz? And what happened to Friedel? This Note on the Author and the Text, written by the de Wind family, is an attempt to answer these and any other questions a reader of *Last Stop Auschwitz* might have.

At the outset it's important to note that Auschwitz was the fulcrum of Eddy de Wind's life, the event upon which everything turned. For him, there was Auschwitz itself, before Auschwitz and after Auschwitz. It overshadowed everything.

Before Auschwitz

Little is known about Eddy's childhood. He became emotionally overwhelmed when the subject was broached, and he would often be overcome by grief for all that had disappeared. We do know that Eliazar de Wind, known as Eddy, was an only child, born on 6 February 1916 in the Piet Heinstraat in The Hague. His mother and father, Henriëtte Sanders and

Louis de Wind, had a number of successful chinaware shops and Eddy was raised in part by nannies. His parents were neither strict nor religious and they paid little heed to the rules of Judaism. Being born into this well-assimilated, prosperous, middle-class Jewish family gave Eddy a good start in life, but when he was just three years old his father died of a brain tumour. More misfortune followed. Around the same time, Eddy pulled a kettle full of boiling water off the work top. He suffered serious burns, spent six months in hospital and was left with large scars on his face and chest.

His mother remarried, but her second husband, Louis van der Stam, also died, in 1936, of a heart attack. Eddy was now twenty and studying medicine at the University of Leiden. When Henriëtte married for a third time, to Louis Zodij, Eddy annoyed him by calling him Louis the Third. Zodij had a twelve-year-old son from a previous marriage, Robert Jacques, who came to live with them. During the Holocaust, Eddy's mother and Louis Zodij were deported to Auschwitz where they were both murdered. Robert Jacques met the same fate.

Because of the events of his childhood, Eddy and his mother developed a close bond. Just how close became clear in 1942, during the war.

Eddy was intelligent and interested in the world around him. Fortunately the setbacks he had suffered in his youth did not prevent him from building a successful social life. In the evenings, for instance, he would regularly meet with friends to discuss world developments. Nietzsche, Freud, Marx and communism were his favourite topics of conversation.

Eddy as a young child with his mother, Henrietta, in 1918.

After completing secondary school, he began studying medicine in Leiden. As he explained it, he had always wanted to be a doctor because he'd had a lot of trouble with asthma as a child and had always loved it when his mother played the doctor. Eddy was a good student and enjoyed life. He had a Christian girlfriend and at night he performed regularly with the Rhythm Rascals, a jazz band in which he played the clarinet. He liked to spend any free days sailing his dinghy.

Eddy with his jazz band the Rhythm Rascals.
He was a talented clarinettist and saxophonist.

Eddy on his sailing boat, before the war.

Both of Eddy's parents came from large Jewish families. Some of his relatives worked in the diamond industry, but most were hard-working people running small businesses. Attending university was still unusual in families such as Eddy's, and they were proud of his achievements.

The de Winds enjoying a celebratory family dinner.
Eddy is standing in the centre at the back.

Although the increasing threat of Nazism had been hanging over the Netherlands from the early thirties, life was looking rosy for Eddy. The German invasion of May 1940 and the occupation of the Netherlands would have come as a terrible shock.

The War

In early 1941 the German occupiers forced the Dutch universities to exclude all Jewish staff and students. With the help of his lecturers at Leiden, Eddy was able to accelerate his studies and he was the last Jewish student to receive a degree. He relocated to Amsterdam to be trained as a psychoanalyst, something that had to be done in secret, in his teachers' homes. He moved into an apartment on the Nieuwe Herengracht, a beautiful, quiet canal near the Jewish quarter, which was home to most of the city's then 80,000 Jews.

The occupiers were tightening the noose around the Jewish community and Eddy became deeply worried. He was convinced that the Germans would put into practice the theories that Hitler had expressed much earlier in *Mein Kampf*. Nonetheless he was surprised when he was arrested. On 22 and 23 February 1941 the Germans rounded up 427 young Jewish men in Amsterdam, Eddy among them. This round-up, the first in the Netherlands, was in retaliation for the death of the Dutch Nazi and paramilitary Hendrik Koot, who was killed in a street battle with Jewish and non-Jewish resistance fighters. Eddy related the events in a 1981 newspaper article in the *NRC Handelsblad*: 'I had gone into town to pick up my bike ... Somewhere in the Jewish quarter I was stopped by a German soldier: "*Bist du Jude?*" Why did I answer, "*Ja.*"? If I'd replied, "Man, are you crazy? Me, a Jew?!" I would have saved my life in that moment, now I had almost certainly thrown it away.'

Together with the other men he was taken to a square between two synagogues, now called the Jonas Daniël Meijerplein, where they had to squat for hours while being beaten by German soldiers. Finally they were carted off in lorries to a prison camp in the small town of Schoorl. After their arrival they were beaten again, harder this time, forced to run the gauntlet while the soldiers hit them with their rifle butts.

For Eddy, the uncertainty and fear were worse than the blows. At that point, he and the other men had no idea what was going to happen to them.

The 427 men were given an 'examination' and those who were too ill were exempted from deportation. Eddy saw an opportunity; just as he would later in Auschwitz, he now benefited from being a doctor. He knew the symptoms of tuberculosis and, helped partly by his asthma, was able to simulate this contagious disease. Together with eleven others who were also considered 'too ill' for the transport, he was released. Running fast and zigzagging through fear of being 'shot while trying to escape', he reclaimed his freedom. The other 415 men were sent to Mauthausen, a hard-labour quarry in Austria. Only two survived the war. Those who were released didn't fare well either. Of the twelve who were declared unfit for transport, Eddy was the only known survivor.

This first round-up led to what was later called 'The February Strike'. Tens of thousands of the people of Amsterdam refused to accept what was happening to 'their' Jews and, under the leadership of the communist party, downed tools. Tram drivers and conductors stopped work. Dock and shipyard workers followed. Factories closed. Shops and offices emptied. It was an act of unprecedented courage. Unfortunately, but inevitably, the strike was violently suppressed.

At the annual commemoration of the February Strike it is always said that only two men survived that first round-up: Max Nebig and Gerrit Blom. Eddy is never mentioned. This is probably because he wasn't one of the 415 who were carted off to Mauthausen, but one of the twelve who were exempted.

*

After his release from Schoorl, Eddy did his best to resume his life. In 1942 things got too hot for him in Amsterdam and he went into hiding with friends of his mother's in The Hague. As he found being cooped up in the house all day very difficult, his host proposed a solution: Eddy should flee to Switzerland. He set out, together with his then fiancée, but at the very first stop, in Antwerp, things went wrong. They couldn't find the house where he was supposed to report, presumably because of an error in the handwritten address. After a few days of searching, the couple were forced to abandon their mission and return to the Netherlands.

This is the story that Eddy would later tell. It is also possible that he sabotaged his flight himself. He had such a strong, deep bond with his mother that, in the end, he might not have been willing to abandon her. Shortly after his return to the Netherlands an event took place that supports this possibility.

Eddy's mother was picked up and taken to Westerbork transit camp. At the same time the Jewish Council, the body that mediated between the occupiers and the Dutch Jews, was looking for Jewish doctors who were willing to work in Westerbork as volunteers. In return for their services, the doctors were given an assurance that they would be allowed to stay there and would not be deported out of the country; they were even allowed to have every second weekend off to visit home as free men. Eddy volunteered for duty on the condition that his mother would be allowed to remain in Westerbork and would not be put on a transport further east. The promise proved worthless. When Eddy arrived in Westerbork a few days later, his mother had already been deported to Auschwitz.

Westerbork was a neatly maintained settlement with a well-functioning administration made up primarily of Jews. There was enough to eat and there were facilities of all kinds, such as a hospital and a theatre. But ultimately, of course, the Nazis were in charge and every week there was a transport with a thousand Jews being shipped off to the east on a freight train. Almost all of them going to the place that was shrouded in rumour and uncertainty, yet feared by almost everyone as possibly their final destination. A place in Poland whose name they only heard on the freight train: Auschwitz.

Eddy was one of the head doctors in Westerbork's small hospital and worked hard. He found one of his tasks unimaginably difficult: he had to 'examine' prisoners who had been named for deportation. Those who were too ill received an exemption. Prisoners were constantly begging him to list friends or relatives as too ill for the transport, but the doctors had to be very cautious as their work was regularly checked by the Germans. It was an impossible task that continued to torment Eddy long after the war, not least because even then some people were still angry with him for not listing a family member as unable to travel.

In the hospital Eddy worked with an eighteen-year-old nurse called Friedel – Frieda – Komornik. Originally from Germany, she had ended up in the camp after an arduous flight. Eddy and Friedel fell in love and he broke off his engagement with his fiancée. To be together they had to marry. That too was possible in Westerbork. For months afterwards, Eddy and Friedel lived in a 'room' that was separated from the hospital ward by a flimsy cardboard partition. It was far from an ideal situation for a newly married couple. But they had each other and were happy enough, given the circumstances. Until fate struck again. Despite the agreements Eddy had made with the Jewish Council, on 14 September 1943 he and Friedel were put on a transport to Auschwitz.

Auschwitz

Immediately after the Germans left Auschwitz, Eddy described his experiences there in the notebook from which the text of this book is reproduced. Sometimes he told his wife and children more about what had happened. He certainly suffered from the feelings of guilt that afflict every survivor: why did I survive when all those others didn't? Besides unimaginable luck, it seems that it was also his love and longing for Friedel that kept him going.

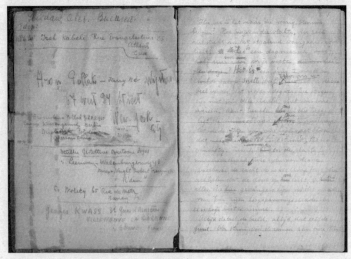

The first page of Eddy's Auschwitz notebook.

A particular strength of *Last Stop Auschwitz* is that it was written during the war and in the camp itself. The text has not been adapted or influenced by changing memories or knowledge that was only gained later, after liberation. This makes the story very honest and gives it great historical value.

It is often extremely confronting. A striking example is the story that Eddy tells about the period when things were going very badly for Friedel. He took it upon himself to speak to the Lagerarzt and asked him to save her life. That seems a ridiculous request in a place where extermination was in large part the reason for its existence, and was the fate of so many of its prisoners, but astonishingly, the Lagerarzt agreed to his request. The story is even more astonishing when you realize the identity of that Lagerarzt: Josef Mengele. It was a name that meant so little to the prisoners at the time that Eddy didn't find it necessary to mention it in his notebook. But it is the name of a man who is now seen as one of the greatest war criminals in history. It is a disturbing thought. Specifically because it makes us realize that the executioners of Auschwitz were not simply beasts or creatures from another planet, but ordinary people, who were capable of making 'humane' decisions.

Does this event make Mengele less evil? Eddy answers this question himself in a conversation he has with Friedel about the inconsistent, seemingly inexplicable way the older members of the SS sometimes made kind decisions. He writes:

> I don't think that's a point in their favour. On the contrary. The youngsters have been raised in the spirit of blood and soil. They don't know any better. But those older ones, like the Lagerarzt, show through those minor acts that they

still harbour a remnant of their upbringing. They didn't learn this inhumanity from an early age and had no need to embrace it. That's why they're guiltier than the young Nazi sheep, who have never known better.

In other words, the fact that Mengele saved Friedel's life, and in doing so showed that he knew what humanity was, makes his behaviour in Auschwitz even more reprehensible.

The book ends with the liberation of Auschwitz in January 1945, but it took several months for the war to be over in the Netherlands too. In that period, Eddy joined the Red Army, who arrived in the camp, and stayed there for a number of months to treat the sick. He then travelled to the rear to help treat the wounded soldiers. In an afterword Eddy wrote for the 1980 republication of the Dutch original of his book, he described what happened:

After the SS had taken the great majority of the prisoners away on death marches to camps deep in Germany, a few thousand people were left behind in the Auschwitz hospital. Within several days of the first Russian troops entering the camp a female medical officer arrived, a major. I was asked to stay in the camp until the last Dutch patients (who managed to stay alive) had been transferred to Russia – and later to Holland. For three months I did all kinds of difficult medical things, carrying out amputations and minor operations, that were actually far beyond my capabilities. I had a busy life and ate copious amounts of American canned chicken and beans. What's more I had found a fur coat in 'Canada' (the storehouse for all Jewish possessions), which I sold at a market ... During the remaining five months in Auschwitz and in Russia I used the money to buy a lot of eggs and cream, so that by the time I returned to Holland in July I had quite a good nutritional status. I don't remember how I was psychologically. The reconstruction of events from so long ago is a precarious business ... I remember very clearly that, shortly after the entry of the Russians, we were taking turns near the gate to dance on a large portrait of Hitler we had found in one of the administrative buildings. I don't recall what I felt while doing so. I suspect that rather than a fine way of venting my hatred, I found it ridiculous ... There was one feeling I definitely had: *I have to let everyone know what happened here. If I record it now and everyone finds out about it, it will never happen again.* At the same time I wanted to leave it all behind me, as if I could liberate myself from all that was haunting me by getting it out and down on the page. An illusion. I got my hands on a very thick note-book, and have it still, in which I wrote an endless account in very small letters every day, sitting on the side of my bed in the former *Polenstube* ... No one can doubt the facts and situations described. This is in contrast to today's books and TV scripts which critics – because of unwillingness or otherwise – can suggest are influenced by the falsification of memories.

Initially uncertain as to whether Friedel was still alive and fearing the worst, on 23 May 1945, soon after the liberation of the Netherlands, Eddy sent a letter from Czernowitz in Ukraine, then part of the Soviet Union, to the Red Cross in the Netherlands. He enclosed a letter to Friedel, in the hope that she might still be alive and that the Red Cross might be able to locate her. It was a letter full of longing and uncertainty.

Czernowitz, 23-5-45

My only love,

All I long for is that you are alive and will receive this letter. I am so scared. But if you are alive, don't worry. I do fear that I won't be home in a hurry, but when I am, we will see each other again at last . . . I long so for you. A couple of months after my liberation I was in a bad state. You had become an obsession to me and I almost turned into a Mussulman, but now I have more of a grip on myself.

I have hope – otherwise I wouldn't be writing this letter –

Now that the Netherlands had finally been liberated he wanted to get there as soon as possible. A long journey through Eastern Europe and over the Mediterranean ensued. Eddy had left the Netherlands in a goods wagon; he returned on a passenger train. From Marseille he travelled through Germany and crossed the Dutch border near the city of Enschede on 24 July 1945. As he didn't have any papers he was taken to a reception centre to be interviewed by a Red Cross worker. He began by giving his personal details, his name and where he had been. And then the miracle happened. The Red Cross worker interrupted him to say that a Mrs de Wind from Auschwitz had returned shortly before him; she was in a near-by hospital. On the day of his return to the Netherlands, Eddy was reunited with Friedel.

After Auschwitz

Friedel and Eddy returned from the war intensely damaged. Eddy's problems were, above all, psychological; Friedel was also very traumatized, but her wounds were physical too. She was infertile and suffered from ill health for many years. Almost all of their family and friends had been murdered and they had no home to return to. It was some time before Eddy and Friedel were able to live together. Initially, she was hospitalized and Eddy lived at the home of his psychiatrist. The Netherlands was so preoccupied with the reconstruction of its infrastructure and society that there was little time for their personal story.

Bravely, Eddy and Friedel picked up their life together. Eddy sold the few family possessions that were left after the war and they used the money to build a house on the outskirts of Amsterdam. Eddy continued his training as a psychoanalyst and began his own practice. But Auschwitz affected everything he did; as a psychoanalyst he specialized in the treatment of people with serious war trauma. As early as 1949 he published his seminal essay 'Confrontation with Death' in which concentration-camp syndrome was described for the first time.

Ultimately Eddy and Friedel's shared suffering and the pain from their trauma proved too great for their relationship. In 1957, twelve years after Auschwitz, they separated.

At drawing lessons Eddy met his second wife, a woman with a very different background. She was from Amsterdam, a good bit younger and not Jewish. They went on to have three children together.

Although energetic and a hard worker, Eddy was regularly overcome by the traumas he carried with him. He was treated at various times, including in the clinic of Jan Bastiaans, the professor of psychiatry who specialized in the treatment of war traumas, where he also underwent experimental treatment with psychedelic drugs to help him process his traumatic past.

The pain and sorrow sometimes came from unexpected directions. Divorcing the wife with whom he had been through so much led some people to think poorly of him. And a section of the Jewish community saw his marriage to a non-Jewish woman as a betrayal. Every year Eddy went to the memorial service of the Dutch Auschwitz Committee. Although many of those present saw him as a hero for dedicating his working life to helping the victims of war, there were some who turned their backs on him because of this 'betrayal'.

As a psychiatrist, Eddy published regularly and was in demand as a speaker at international conferences, specifically concerning the later consequences of war trauma. He was also successful in his second speciality, sexology, helping to found the first Dutch abortion clinic and publishing a survey of sexual preferences entitled *Variation or Perversion*.

Later in his life Eddy understood increasingly that traumas do not cease to exist with those directly involved, but that survivors pass them on to their children. He set up a foundation to gather research into and knowledge of this subject, the *Stichting Onderzoek Psychische Oorlogsgevolgen* or SOPO (the 'Foundation for the Investigation of the Psychological Consequences of War'). It was an ambitious project in which he was able to engage many international specialists.

In 1984, three years before his death, he was given a royal honour by being made an Officer in the Order of

Orange-Nassau, something he saw as more than just recognition of the good work he had done. For him the honour was an acknowledgement of his survival having had a purpose.

While working on SOPO, Eddy suffered a severe heart attack. A difficult period followed in which he grew weaker and weaker.

His confrontation with his approaching death took him back to Auschwitz and he fell victim to terrible fears and nightmares. After more than a month of illness his damaged heart failed completely. Eddy died on 27 September 1987 at the age of seventy-one.

© Jeroen van Amelrooij

Eddy de Wind at seventy, a year before his death.

A Note on this Publication

After his return to the Netherlands, Eddy realized that most people were so happy that the war was over that, after an initial flurry, there was little interest in his stories about the death camps. Reconstruction was the priority. Nonetheless he decided to persevere with his resolution to let people know what had happened so that it could never happen again, and it wasn't long before his story was published. The text about his experiences in Auschwitz, which he had written in the space of a few weeks sitting on the side of his wooden bed in the camp, was adopted virtually word for word and at the start of 1946 *Last Stop Auschwitz* was published by the communist publisher De Republiek der Letteren, with the title *Eindstation Auschwitz*. Unfortunately the publisher went bankrupt shortly after the book came out and it was only available to the general public for a short period and soon forgotten. Among Dutch survivors, however, the book has long been treasured as one of the most important on Auschwitz.

Consumed by the reconstruction of his own life, Eddy decided to leave the book for the time being. It wasn't until 1980 that he made a new attempt at its publication and a complete reprint appeared with the publisher Van Gennep. Eddy's motivation for republishing was a sombre one, as he was increasingly concerned about what he had hoped would never happen: a revival of intolerance and political violence, including in the West.

Rather than being merely a historical report and a reckoning with what had happened, he saw *Last Stop Auschwitz* as a universal story illustrating how some people can continue to support and love each other even under the most extreme circumstances, retaining a certain freedom of their mental faculties, as well as a story that shows how intolerance and an extreme sense of superiority can lead to the most unimaginable deeds.

The 1980 edition of the book was successful but, much to Eddy's disappointment, the publisher failed to keep the book in print. This is not to say that Eddy put it out of his head. He still realized that it was important for everyone to read what had happened in Auschwitz, and he worked on an English translation of his story until shortly before his death.

Seventy-five years after the liberation of Auschwitz, Eddy's original notebook is now being exhibited all over the world and the book is being published worldwide. It is a tribute to all those who have suffered under terror and political violence. It is also the fulfilment of the wish Eddy expressed at the end of his story: 'I have to stay alive to tell all of this, to tell everyone about it, to convince people that it was true ...'

This Note on the Author and the Text includes a section of the afterword that Eddy de Wind wrote for the 1980 republication of *Last Stop Auschwitz* in the Netherlands. Further use has been made of various sources, including texts from Eddy de Wind's notebook that were not included in the original publication of *Last Stop Auschwitz*, Red Cross archives, the archives of the Auschwitz-Birkenau State Museum, as well as the article by Eddy published in the *NRC Handelsblad* of 14 February 1981.

The de Wind family
Amsterdam, August 2019

'Confrontation with Death'
by Eddy de Wind

THE DUTCH ORIGINAL OF this article was first published in *Folia psychiatrica, neurologica et neurochirurgica Neerlandica* vol. 52 (1949), December, 459–66. It was first published in English, in a different translation, in the *International Journal of Psycho-Analysis* vol. 49 (1968), 302–5.

Immediately after liberation, people were keen to read everything that was published about the concentration camps. Even in those early days, some writers tried to make sociological and psychological conclusions in their work. The public devoured it all uncritically, but soon became sated. Financial worries, fears of new global catastrophes and, above all, disillusionment about post-war relations dulled people's interest. At the same time, it is not pleasant to be constantly reminded of the suffering of others, while also feeling as if one is being held responsible because of real or alleged failings regarding those who have died or undergone great hardship.

I would spare the listeners all of the horror stories about the camps, if it were not for the fact that we – the former inmates – are still astonished every day by how little is known in the Netherlands about what happened there, especially in Polish camps like Auschwitz. Those who wrote about their experiences shortly after liberation did it mainly to try to find some peace of mind. By writing about the camps, one conquered one's pent-up emotions. It is understandable that readers, who had to take over this burden, soon had enough of it, and the interest for camp literature began to wane. Unfortunately, people threw the baby out with the bathwater by failing to subject the former inmates' academic conclusions to closer inquiry.

Several years have now passed and the memory of the camp is beginning to lose some of its torturous, affective character. What was once the most hideous reality now seems like a horror film we saw in our childhood years. Fear and rage still rush at us together with the remembered images, but they are like wild animals that have been caged . . . They can no longer pounce, we have distanced ourselves from them.

Thanks to this distancing we can consider what we experienced more objectively. We no longer feel caught up in the atmosphere of the camp, but think about how to convey it at our desks, studying it the way a chemist observes reactions in test tubes. We see the camp with its streets and barracks, and inside them – as reagents – the people. We let the circumstances affect them and watch the way they change. The experiment takes place . . .

We are familiar with many of the Germans' experiments: dermatological, surgical and numerous others. I have studied the protocols (in Nuremberg), which the '*SS Lagerärzte*' wrote for Brandt, the 'Führer's' personal physician . . . I shall spare you the horrors. But there was one experiment I couldn't find any report of, the experiment 'Camp'. The Germans are not aware of the meaning of the camp as a social-psychological experiment. It is up to us now to draw up these protocols.

Much has been written about man in mortal danger. I remember the well-known publication in which Dr M. G. Vroom describes the experience of deadly peril during bombing raids. In this situation, however, and also for troops at the front, the threat of death has a different meaning than it does for the inmates of a camp. For the former the threat is acute, whereas for the latter it is chronic and, unlike soldiers who have a sense of fighting for their lives, prisoners are also defenceless.

We immediately think of the experiences of Dostoyevsky, which he – autobiographically – describes for us in *The Idiot*:

> But in the case of an execution, that last hope – having which it is so immeasurably less dreadful to die – is taken away from the wretch and *certainty* substituted in its place! There is his sentence, and with it that terrible certainty that he cannot possibly escape death – which, I consider, must be the most dreadful anguish in the world. You may place a soldier before a cannon's mouth in battle, and fire upon him – and he will still hope. But read to that same soldier his death-sentence, and he will either go mad or burst into tears. Who dares to say that any man can suffer this *without going mad*?*

Later in *The Idiot* we read about a condemned man who is standing on the scaffold: 'What should I do if I were not to die now? What if I were to return to life again? . . . He said that this thought weighed so upon him and became such a terrible

* Translated by Eva Martin. Italics, Eddy de Wind.

burden upon his brain that he could not bear it, and *wished they would shoot him quickly and have done with it.*'*

Running through these quotes, we see two lines of thought.

First, that it seemed inconceivable to Dostoyevsky that someone could have the certainty of a death sentence and not go insane.

Second, that as soon as death has become a certainty, the tension becomes so unbearable that one longs for death as the only escape from the tension.

Of the four and a half million Jews who arrived in Auschwitz, four thousand at most (one per thousand) survived.† Most of those who died knew the inevitability of death. Nonetheless, they did not go mad. Let us investigate how that was possible. To understand the thoughts and emotions of camp inmates confronted with death, we need to review what the Jews had been through before their deportation to Auschwitz.

In Amsterdam and in Westerbork, for instance, the mentality of the Jews was characterized by a tremendous repression of reality. Despite the fact that everyone could rationally understand that they too would one day be compelled to make the journey to Poland, everyone convinced themselves that *they* would avoid it, and the gassing in Poland (discussed on BBC radio as early as 1941) was something people simply didn't want to hear about; reality was fobbed off with the words 'British propaganda'. It was only when they were on a train crossing the Dutch border that everyone

---

* Translated by Eva Martin. Italics, Eddy de Wind.
† It is not known exactly how many people were sent to Auschwitz or how many died there. Historians tend to estimate that around 1.3 million people were sent to the camp and that 1.1 million people were murdered there.

realized just how fictitious the sense of security that had been maintained with Jewish Council stamps and all kinds of German lists and other assurances had been.

Because of this repression of reality and their fictitious sense of security, the great majority of Dutch Jews never made any attempt to save themselves through flight or resistance, as opposed to Jews such as those in the Warsaw Ghetto, who were realists with centuries of training in resistance to anti-Semitism.

The Germans cunningly promoted this process of repression in the Netherlands by making Westerbork a 'good' camp, where many facilities were provided.

Deportation still remained inevitable and when, on the train to Poland, repression became unsustainable, another defence mechanism took effect: people succumbed to a hypomanic mood. The crowd was like a frightened child who sings in the dark to hide his fear. One pulled out a guitar, a second started to sing, infecting a third with his cheerfulness, and soon the whole cattle-truck was singing along. The perversely cheerful mood was intensified by the sight of bombed cities in Germany and, consciously at least, the fear of the camp disappeared completely.

When the train then stopped for a long time in the yards at the railway station of the town of Auschwitz, there was only one longing: to set off again and reach the camp as quickly as possible. Nobody realized that this arrival would probably be their end …

After many hours the train started rolling again, only to stop soon afterwards at a long embankment in the green countryside. Standing on the embankment were shaven-headed men in striped convict uniforms. As the train pulled up they rushed over to the wagons and jerked open the doors.

In that instant the repression was still in effect. A doctor who had made the journey in the same wagon as me with his wife and child remarked, 'Look, they're prisoners from a concentration camp. They have to help us with our baggage.'

This man was like a tourist on a merry mountain hike who is oblivious to all danger until the avalanche comes crashing down on him. Arrival in a concentration camp is a severe psychic trauma akin to being buried by an avalanche. The facts rush at the newcomers so fast that they are in danger of being crushed by them.

Eighty per cent of the travellers were loaded on to large lorries. These were the old, the invalids and the mothers with children. They were taken to the '*Bad- und Desinfektionsraum*'. There, in the hermetically sealed washroom, they were summoned by loudspeaker to breathe in deeply to disinfect the lungs of contagious diseases. What went through these people's minds in the instant they realized that the gas was poisonous is something we can scarcely imagine. As cruel as their fate was, it would be too speculative to go into their emotions during the moment of stupefaction . . .

We will follow the others, the strong young people, closely.

The psychic trauma took place in several phases. After the doors of the goods wagons had been thrown open, the prisoners drove the travellers out with sticks and cudgels. For the first time the new arrivals discovered how people are treated in a concentration camp, not just by the SS, but also by some categories of prisoners with long experience of camp life. In Auschwitz these were mostly Poles.

Then all the baggage had to be thrown on to a pile and one said goodbye to the last material possessions one had brought from home. But what followed was worst of all. Long lines were formed on the embankment: the line for the elderly, the young men's line and the young women's. People now realized the inevitable, that they were going to be split up and would have to go through a long, fearful period of uncertainty before seeing each other again.

But in that instant, people still believed that they would be reunited later and called out a sincere 'till we meet again'.

As the rows set in motion, the multiple psychic traumas continued step by step.

After passing a barrier, the line of young men entered the grounds of the actual camp.

Storage yards for building supplies, large ramshackle sheds and enormous stacks of bricks and timber. There were small trains, propelled by hand power, and large wagons pulled by fifteen to twenty men, all dressed in prison uniforms. Here and there along the road there were factories with the hum of machinery coming from the inside, then more timber, bricks and sheds. There was life everywhere and everywhere buildings were being built.

The newcomers began to make associations with descriptions of forced labour in previous centuries – galley slaves and convicts – and then came the incomprehensible thought, now I am a convict too. Things one had only known from books – Dostoyevsky's *House of the Dead* – and from the film *I Am a Fugitive from a Chain Gang* suddenly became reality.

Then the lads were at the gate and seeing the camp they would have to live in for the first time. Above the gate, in decorative cast iron, the concentration camp slogan: '*ARBEIT MACHT FREI*'.

A suggestion designed to reconcile the thousands who would enter here to their fate, by offering them a glimmer of hope.

Keeping that hope alive until the last moment was part of the camp system. Besides perhaps in individual threats, the SS never admitted that extermination was the goal. Artificially launched rumours seeped through the crowded camp like an anaesthetic poison, feeding irrational illusions and keeping the prisoners from active resistance. The suggestion that work would set you free was soon rendered ineffective by the first conversations with more senior camp residents, among them some of our compatriots.

The truth about the tortures, infectious diseases, starvation and especially the weekly recurring 'selections', in which the weakest were picked out and taken to the gas chambers, was flung mercilessly in the newcomers' faces.

I remember speaking to a Dutchman – perhaps an hour after my arrival in the camp. He was a strong, well-built young man, who also looked well nourished. He predicted that none of us would get out alive. I still clung to him: 'How long have *you* been here then?'

'A year.'

'But then it must be bearable!'

Unfortunately, the Dutchman wasted no time in shattering my illusions by telling me that he was the last survivor from his transport of one thousand people. He was a champion boxer and the SS appreciated his boxing skills so much that they had taken him under their wing.

In this way we soon knew very precisely which fate was in store for us. The exhausting work, the meagre daily rations and the lack of rest already made it clear to us that camp life was unbearable. And when we first saw the wagons with the most exhausted prisoners leaving for Birkenau, the part of the camp with the crematoria, there was no more room for doubt. Although our rational minds were convinced, irrational hope remained. Hope was mainly nourished by the rumours, which were, in turn, fed by hope, but besides this there were also peculiar facts: for instance, many of the prisoners worked in Krupp and IG Farben factories and in the so-called 'Deutsche Ausrüstungswerkstatte'. There they were given certain privileges: an extra half-litre of soup and sometimes extra bread, a straw mattress to themselves that they didn't need to share with two or three other men. Sometimes they even got 'pay', a 'Prämienschein' of one mark, which they could use to buy onions in the canteen, or lavatory paper, an enormous luxury.

If we spoke to the older prisoners about these facts, they only responded with a sneer. They knew all too well how it would end. Nonetheless they had to admit that something had changed in the camp, and when we sometimes bemoaned our fate, they mocked us. 'You have no idea what a camp is. Compared to our day it's a sanatorium here now.' We were constantly hurled back and forth from hope to dread, from emotional, irrational hope to reasoned dread, the virtual certainty that this would all mean the end.

This mixture of conflicting responses is not that strange. It is familiar to everyone. But in the camp the divergence was so strong, there was such a distance between thought and emotion, that it was scarcely possible to speak of a mixture any more. It was so overwhelming that there were two consciousnesses living in each person – one knowing and the other hoping – moving independently of each other and having virtually no influence on each other.

The certainty of the approaching end gave rise to a numbed resignation, but in those urgent moments when a prisoner was in danger of succumbing, the quiet hope was a stimulus to hold out a little longer.

In this way one always lasted a little longer in the camp than one could have lasted according to human calculations.

The six phases of the confrontation with the concentration camp had the effect of an equal number of psychic traumas: the confiscation of the baggage, the separation of the families, the impressions of the people working outside the camp, the sight of the camp with its electrified barbed wire, the shaving and the tattooing with the *Häftlingsnummer* and, above all, the newcomers' communications with the senior prisoners are comparable to the most intense traumas we see in the field of traumatic neuroses. And the reaction to these traumas was the same as the reaction to an intense, acute shock: the result was a stuporous condition. Stupor characterized the prisoners' behaviour in the first weeks. They were quiet and inhibited, and unable to understand the snarled orders in concentration camp jargon.

They found it impossible to get the soup, which they would later crave, down their throats, and the slowness of their reactions made an extremely stupid impression on the more senior prisoners and especially the SS. This was the '*blödes Schwein*' stage in which many perished. When they failed to properly follow the orders they had not understood, they were beaten to death, or their awkward behaviour resulted in their being assigned to the heaviest *Kommandos*, where they had to carry out unbearable labour. There were also some, though these were the least in number, who showed a different attitude right from the start. They refused to bend the knee and behaved fairly arrogantly, trying to withstand the law of the concentration camp with their iron will and by putting on a show of bravery. They too soon went under. Rather than '*blöd*', they were '*frech*' and those who were *frech* were also beaten to death, albeit for other reasons than the *Blöde*. Still there were also some who, after a short while, managed to find an attitude that made it possible to bear the camp over a longer period thanks to a peculiar kind of adaptation, which is such an interesting phenomenon that I would like to take it as an additional subject for this study. And although I realize that what I will now say is still very incomplete and in many points disputable, I believe nonetheless that I have sufficient material to justify elaborating my chain of thought for you. To immediately give you a picture of a prisoner who found the right style, I will read you a passage from the case history of a patient who spent a long time in camps and recently came to me because of the difficulties he is having adapting.

The patient said the following: 'I don't understand myself how I came through it. Of the four hundred men who were transported to Buna with me, only thirty were left after a year. I always just let myself go. When the Kapo hit me, I thought, just beat me to death. When there was a bombing raid, I thought, if only I'm lucky enough to be hit by a bomb. I was completely apathetic. When the Dutch lads spoke to me, I thought, ah, just let them talk, and couldn't follow the conversation. The Kapo said, "I don't understand why you're not in the crematorium yet." I shirked work as much as I could and if they noticed, they'd sometimes beat me to the ground; I didn't care. In the end I didn't feel the blows any more. I didn't bleed from them any more either. Once during a selection I was written down, standing among dozens of Mussulmen. The next day I presented to the Lagerarzt, who asked me what my profession was. I said "warehouseman". If I'd said "diamond cutter", I'd have been gone. They always said, "All you Jews are good for is cutting diamonds and doing business." On an impulse, I answered "warehouseman".'

In this man we see a remarkable capacity to let insult and injury pass him by virtually unnoticed. Later we even heard from him that eventually he almost found it pleasant to be tormented. The line from Exodus we can find on the urn tomb in Westerbork is applicable to him: 'Pure oil from olives, beaten, beaten and pounded, to bear suffering as light.'

Although I can't go too deeply into the theoretical background of this capacity to 'bear suffering as light', I would like to draw several parallels and would primarily recall what Freud has described for us in 'Beyond the Pleasure Principle', although it's certainly not necessary to quote Freud in this company. And we are also familiar with just how much the death drive Freud posits in that essay is still a moot point. Nonetheless we must admit that people like the patient I have just described had adapted strongly to the idea of dying. And in their cases we can clearly apply the opinion of Carp,* who puts it a little more broadly when he says that people whose individual earthly existence has become unbearable because of certain tensions long for a resolution of this existence and a continuation in another. And is it not abundantly clear that the stupor we have described in the newcomers was a consequence of this death principle? The

---

* Eugène Carp (1895–1983) was a prominent professor of psychology in the Netherlands.

prisoner who had actually given up on life under the influence of psychic trauma had reconciled himself to the idea of dying. He was certain that he would one day get out of the camp, but believed – to express it in concentration camp terms – that it would be '*durch den Kamin*', by way of the crematorium chimney; or, in other words, 'I will definitely get out, if not horizontally, vertically.' The prisoner was like a Raskolnikov.* He sought misery and humiliation. For him, blows and hunger were no longer traumas but aids to achieve his goal: death. If this condition continued, death would be the result. If the prisoner did not get beaten to death, he would die from disease, and it was apparent that the exceptionally florid tubercular processes we saw in the camp were exacerbated by a desire to die.

We have seen that the man who surrendered completely to the camp soon perished, but the man who resisted with all his vitality exhausted his energies quickly as well, using up his mental and physical reserves in a futile struggle against the law of '*l'univers concentrationnaire*'. This brings us to the paradox that reconciling oneself to death was a vital condition for the prisoner, that it was necessary for him to submit, and that his only chance of staying alive was if he, alongside this submission, which really can be called a form of inner acceptance, retained sufficient vitality to give the right answer at critical moments, just as our patient, who had let himself go completely, answered 'warehouseman' instead of 'diamond cutter' in the moment when the *Lagerarzt* was choosing his victims for the gas chambers.

* Rodion Romanovich Raskolnikov is the fictional protagonist of Fyodor Dostoyevsky's 1866 novel *Crime and Punishment*.

Compared to ordinary life, staying alive in the camp required a different relationship between vitality and what I – to avoid discussions about the term 'death drive' – would like to call the death principle. Whereas in ordinary life vitality generally has the upper hand and the death principle only dominates in pathological conditions such as melancholy, its domination in the concentration camp was a necessity. To summarize I can say that the stuporous prisoner who was completely dominated by the death principle perished from it, as did those who resisted the camp with all their vitality. The prisoner who wanted to have a chance of life had to develop a certain camp psyche, the deeper basis of which was an altered attitude to death.

Let us now analyse the factors that made the emergence of such a camp psyche possible. In the first instance several physical factors.

Various experiences, particularly in the last war, have made it clear how much deficiencies play a role in the decline of mental function. This decline is not regular, but selective. The vitamin B complex in particular seems to play a role. During the autopsies carried out by Russian doctors on prisoners who had died after liberation, I saw very remarkable abnormalities. The intestinal wall had become as thin as parchment, which was explained as epithelium loss from B deficiency. In cerebro we saw petechiae, a presentation similar to that of Wernicke encephalopathy, and although there is still a shortage of facts regarding deficiency psychoses, I would like to draw attention to experiments by American researchers who evoked psychotic states by putting experimental subjects on a diet that was low in vitamin B6, niacin. May I also draw attention to Grewel's description of 'anaemia perniciosa', not a direct result of malnutrition, but nonetheless a deficiency disease:

> Speed of action and resilience decline. The same applies to thought processes. Psychological tone is reduced ... Sometimes there are over-sensitivities, including to pain and emotions ... Apathy alternates with fits of anger, irritability and affectability.

It is apparent that these few facts require further study. Nonetheless I am convinced that we will gain the most not from studies of the prisoners' physical conditions, but by paying particular attention to the sociological conditions in which they lived. And this brings us to the second group of factors that give rise to the development of a camp psyche.

The word 'sociological' may sound inflated, until one realizes that a conglomeration of tens of thousands – up to as many as 200,000 people, as in Auschwitz-Birkenau – cannot simply be seen as an unstructured crowd. Instead, various social ranks operated within this mass and could not but influence the psychological condition of the individuals.

In order to explain the social relations in the concentration camps, I must first summarize several facts from the history of these camps. The first ones were set up in 1933: small camps with two to three hundred prisoners each. These had a purely political function in relation to the Nazi takeover. In addition they were a practising ground for SS methods. The SS was trained there for its later task of European domination.

Around the start of the war, the camps' second function developed. The mass extermination of the Jews became an economic necessity for the German conduct of the war. This led to the large death camps Majdanek and Treblinka, and the largest, Auschwitz. But once such enormous SS cities had arisen, it turned out that these could also fulfil a further function. In

1937 Pohl, who was in charge of the economic side of the camps, uttered his historic words: '*Warum sollte die SS nichts verdienen*',* and increasingly from then on, the camps became enormous factories in which the prisoners laboured as brutally exploited workers.

Initially all of the prisoners in the camps were treated equally badly, but gradually a separate class arose among them of prisoners favoured by the SS, the Kapos and *Blockälteste*, who served as an extension of the SS and allowed them to put as many prisoners as possible to work. In 1937 the first public limited companies in concentration camps were created. The shareholders were ... members of the SS. During the war important branches of German industrial concerns (Krupp, IG Farben) were established in the camps. The prisoners were hired from the SS for six marks a day. In his book *The Theory and Practice of Hell*, Kogon† calculated that the profit per prisoner per day was approximately four marks, which across all camps came to hundreds of thousands of marks a day, and billions over the whole war. After all, nine and a half million people died there,‡ of whom approximately forty per cent produced several months of profit for the SS.

As long as there were enough Jews and political adversaries in all of the countries of Europe, the SS was reckless with prisoners' lives. But around 1943 the supply began to dwindle and it therefore became necessary to relax the regime in the camps

* 'Why shouldn't the SS earn anything?'
† *The Theory and Practice of Hell: The German concentration camps and the system behind them* by Eugen Kogon (New York: Berkley Books, 1950).
‡ It is generally estimated by historians that between 5 and 6 million people died in the Holocaust, in camps, and also by execution and as a result of disease.

to safeguard war production and SS profiteering. This gave the prisoners a little breathing space. We see that the SS had two contradictory goals with its prisoners: on the one hand, rapid and efficient mass extermination; on the other, sparing them for the economic benefit they could generate. In 1944 this split in the mentality of the camp reached a climax with the double function of death camp and economically essential labour camp. The remarkable tension that existed in the prisoners between surrendering to death and their constantly recurring bursts of vitality, the inner ambivalence, being thrown back and forth between hope and dread, was sustained by its emotional resonance with the split nature of the social environment.

This already indicates a likely link between two apparently independent phenomena: the sociological structure of the camp and the prisoners' psychic structure. We see how a social form that is essentially different from any society we know can also cause psychological changes of a depth we could not have previously suspected. It goes without saying that there is important individual variation in the ability to adjust to the camp environment by developing the psychic state described above. There was a great difference between the reactions of Eastern European Jews with their strong Slavic streak, who had been accustomed to anti-Semitism from an early age, and those of Western Jews. When it came to the Dutch, the Jewish proletarians – the orange vendor from Waterloo Square and the cigar maker from Uilenburg – were made of sterner stuff than members of the prosperous middle class, whose entire facade of self-importance collapsed at the first blow or swear word, at least when they had no deeper source of self-esteem than their social position. In general in the camp we saw that those whose lives had some kind of religious alignment (this in the broadest sense, also as a devotion to a political system or a humanistic philosophy) were the quickest to recover from the initial stupor. It is therefore no coincidence that both the faithful Christians and those who would seem to be their psychological opposites, the communists, were best at holding their own in the camp and even found opportunities to achieve some degree of anti-fascist organization. The same phenomenon was seen in the Dutch resistance with the close-knit groups around the underground newspapers *Trouw* and *De Waarheid*.

Of course the adaptive mechanisms described above did not apply to the ruling group among the prisoners, the Kapos and *Blockälteste*, often sadists and psychopaths and as bad as the SS buddies they drank with and joined in visits to the brothel. But of those prisoners who suffered the full misery of the camp, it can be said that, inasmuch as they managed to stick it out, it was because they had so deeply reconciled themselves to the idea of going under and because the normally dominant vital urge only manifested itself incidentally, in truly critical moments. A small reserve of this will to live could be kept for those moments because in the background of consciousness the thought remained alive that existence might have another meaning than just making it through another day.

Even now, years after the war, we regularly see how difficult it is to reverse the far-reaching alteration of personality that took place in the camps. For this reason it seems to me that an insight into the living conditions that formed the people in the camps, which I have sketched briefly above, is a necessary prerequisite if we are to offer help to the dis-equilibrated former prisoners who visit our practices.

Translator's Note

A LITERARY TRANSLATOR SHOULD BE faithful, everyone knows that, but people often don't realize that faithfulness operates on many levels and that these levels sometimes conflict with each other. Strict adherence to the meaning might, for instance, hobble the elegance of the original or block the associations that make it so evocative. Still other factors come into play in *Last Stop Auschwitz*, which was written explicitly as a testimony and needs to be respected not just as a personal and political account, but also as part of the historical record.

Eddy de Wind's book is remarkable for many reasons, not just the horrors he describes and his early insights into the political and psychological processes of totalitarianism, but also the conditions under which he wrote it. His having found the energy, drive and commitment to write a book like this in the evenings after spending long days carrying out difficult medical procedures is beyond admirable. Inevitably the circumstances led to a certain roughness and lack of structure, but this only adds to the book's rawness and authenticity. *Last Stop Auschwitz* is a report from the belly of the beast. The SS had been driven away and the camp had been liberated, but de Wind was still inside the monster, fighting to save the lives of its victims.

In his afterword to the 1980 republication of the 1946 Dutch original, de Wind explains that a well-known publisher was interested in taking the book on, but wanted it to be rewritten first. Instead de Wind kept looking and found a smaller, more political publisher who preferred a new edition that was 'as faithful to the original as possible'. De Wind was happy to agree, even though he realized that doing so might expose him to 'criticism for the style and immature political statements'. To his mind, this risk was more than compensated by 'the greater guarantee of authenticity'.

Returning to the levels of faithfulness in translation, *Last Stop Auschwitz* requires a certain inversion of the usual practice. If a translator generally strives to make their translation as polished as the original, here an aspect of faithfulness is trying to retain the rawness of the original rather than producing something more like an English version of the rewritten book De Wind himself rejected. There is a contradiction here, because translation *is* 'rewriting', rewriting in another language, but while doing so I have done my best to retain the rough edges of the original and with them its directness and urgency. I wanted it to be good English, of course, but English that was as much like the Dutch as possible.

An important exception is the spelling of names. In his notebook De Wind often approximated the spelling of names or wrote them down phonetically, presumably because he had only heard them and never seen them written down, or had seen them and forgotten the spelling. It's no surprise that the original Dutch publisher didn't have the resources for extensive fact checking in the immediate postwar period, but at that time, when the Nuremberg trials had only just begun and knowledge of the camps was still relatively limited, it would have also been extremely difficult to obtain information that is now just a few clicks away. As interested readers will soon discover, it is not difficult to find additional information online about many of the historical figures named in the book. It was only natural, then, to correct 'Glauberg' to 'Clauberg', 'Klausen' to 'Claussen' and 'Döring' to 'Dering'.

A final point to clarify is my treatment of De Wind's use of foreign languages. The concentration camps were a confusing multilingual environment with German as the language of command and authority, but often spoken by non-German prisoners. In general, my approach was to translate De Wind's Dutch into English and reproduce his use of other languages, but, as usual with translation, it wasn't always that simple. De Wind often mixes Dutch and German, for instance, perhaps reflecting the way the Dutch prisoners spoke in the camp, and at least once he uses a German word in a sense that seems specifically Dutch, and therefore not really German at all.

The German content in the book is significant: both the short lines of dialogue spoken in German and the multitude of terms relating to the SS and the concentration camps. Again I have corrected any obvious mistakes, while trying to bear in mind Primo Levi's description of the corruption of the German language in the camps and his account in *The Drowned and the Saved* of his otherwise excellent German translator's consistent inclination to turn Levi's remembered camp German into something he, as a German-speaker, considered more plausible. Reading about Levi's correspondence with his translator made me realize once again how much of a shame it is that this book wasn't translated thirty or fifty or sixty years ago when the author could have been consulted and would, later, have been able to hold the English edition in his hand as further proof that there *was* a purpose to his survival.

David Colmer
Amsterdam, August 2019

EDDY DE WIND (1916–87) was the last Jewish doctor to graduate from Leiden University in the Netherlands during World War Two. He volunteered to work at the Westerbork labour camp under the false impression that his mother, who had been taken by the Germans, would be saved from deportation. There, he met and married his first wife, Friedel. The couple was deported to Auschwitz in 1943.

De Wind returned to Holland in the summer of 1945 and specialized as a psychiatrist and psychoanalyst. In 1949 he published 'Confrontation with Death', his famous article in which he introduced the idea of concentration-camp syndrome. *Last Stop Auschwitz* was published in Dutch in February 1946. As far as is known, it is the only complete book written in Auschwitz itself.